To Tom Petreg
    Christmas 1997

With Best Wishes.
    From Mum + Dad W.

REFLECTIONS
OF A COUNTRYMAN

Fred J. Taylor

REFLECTIONS
OF A
COUNTRYMAN

White Lion Books
CAMBRIDGE

White Lion Books
an imprint of
Colt Books Ltd
9 Clarendon Road
Cambridge CB2 2BH
TEL: 01223 357047 FAX: 01223 365866

This new edition first published by White Lion Books 1997

First published by Stanley Paul in 1982

Text Copyright © Fred J. Taylor 1982 and 1997
Foreword copyright © Tony Jackson 1997

Jacket front illustration is by Denys Watkins-Pitchford
from *The Fisherman's Bedside Book*

Jacket design by Clare Byatt

ISBN 1 874762 36 8

Printed in Great Britain by Biddles Ltd

Contents

To Carrie:
for her love and patience

Foreword

How may of us, I wonder, at the age of 78 would have spent last winter camping in the bush in Canada or be planning to head for Egypt "to try a little fishing and see where I spent the entire war as a Desert Rat"?

Fred J. Taylor is overweight, enjoys his food, drinks in moderation and, as you will come to discover as you read this delightful book, rejoices in life to the full. He claims that the secret of his enduring powers, as a countryside writer and practising sportsman, is that he is fortunate to know so many young people. That is as maybe, for I think they are fortunate to know him.

I've been lucky enough to have worked with Fred for nearly 25 years, since he first wrote for me in 1973 when I edited *Shooting Times*, and we still often collaborate. He is that increasingly rare creature, a true countryman, one who takes interest in every aspect of the rural scene and one who knows it with a deep and abiding understanding.

Reflections of a Countryman is more than just a series of rural vignettes, it is the life story of one of the great country writers of this century, for I class Fred J. Taylor with Hudson, Eric Parker, the neglected Frances Pitt and with 'BB', the late Denys Watkins-Pitchford. The secret of their success was that they knew their subjects from every angle and, furthermore, they could write clear, simple prose.

This is where Fred, a seemingly simple soul... apparently at his most content when grubbing after rabbits, fishing for pike in a cold dawn or just sitting by a camp-fire under the stars... is master of an art which few acquire though many, mistakenly, think they do. His writing is compelling and though you may, perhaps, think his stories of country life are unadorned, almost ingenuous, each is crafted with all the loving care of a master.

Read this charming volume and you will find yourself embroiled in the real, living countryside, not the stuff of television or of earnest, bearded young men whose learning comes from academia. Here is Fred poaching pheasants with raisins soaked in brandy, shooting with a desperate old muzzle-loader, fishing through the ice in Minneapolis or spot-lamping rabbits in his beloved Australia. Always you, the reader, are by his side as he unfolds his tale of adventure, however minor. This is the secret of good writing.

Enjoy this new edition of *Reflections of a Countryman* and offer praise that Fred is still amongst us and, God willing, will be entertaining us for many a year to come.

Tony Jackson
July, 1997

Preface

In a lifetime's involvement with field sports generally there has been much to learn. I have not learnt it all. If I thought I had, I would no longer wish to remain a field sportsman. I have learned,.however, to become reasonably proficient at reaping some of nature's harvests in different parts of the world. I was obviously born to be a 'hunter' and in the main I have been motivated by the desire to hunt for food. I have always regarded it as foolish not to take annual crops, but sinful to overexploit them, and these beliefs have made me recognize the need for conservation. I am a conservationist but not a preservationist. There is a difference and I believe I am fortunate in being able to recognize it.

Some of what I have learned is disclosed in the pages that follow but it would take a hundred such books and another lifetime to tell it all. Only so much may be included here, much has to be omitted and one is tempted always to relate the most spectacular, to record the special days and leave out those occasions when plans did not succeed. I have tried to avoid falling into this trap and to record the happenings as I remember them. Spectacular events are often forgotten because they hold no lasting value, and I have tried to record those events that were of interest to me. Even so I have been able to include only a small percentage. Much has transpired since the manuscript was finished and the temptation to add more chapters has been hard to resist. But somewhere there has to be an end and in the meantime I know that I shall go on learning.

I have been encouraged to follow my chosen course by many kind friends and associates, and I thank them all here for their help and guidance. It would take too long to name them all but they will know – and remember.

My thanks are due to the editors of *Shooting Times and Country Magazine*, the *Standard*, the *Sunday Telegraph* and *Anglers' Mail* for permission to include extracts from previously published articles in the following pages.

Fred J. Taylor

Introduction

When I was young I imagined myself as a bit of a poacher. I trespassed and I took game and rabbits, shot birds with airguns, and I caught hundreds in cotton nooses one at a time until I had enough for one of mother's pies. Seasons meant little to me and I reaped the harvests of moorhen eggs, coot eggs, mallard eggs and all the other kinds of edible goodies I could lay my hands upon, while watching out for the ever-vigilant keeper. I will not try to pretend that I was one of those sly characters who poached game nightly and who were always able to outwit the keepers who lay in wait for them. Things might have been sticky on occasions had I been caught, but I was never greedy and I never pushed my luck. I didn't really enjoy poaching, except, perhaps, for the night-time excitement. I never walked with gun across land where I'd no right to be and, apart from shooting over a boundary fence occasionally (which the best of sportsmen sometimes still do today), I used more silent methods.

My father and uncles were poachers – though they never admitted it. They had permission to kill rabbits and vermin here and there, but if the truth be told they probably strayed a little, and without doubt the odd hare or partridge came their way.

The legality of some of their long-netting operations at night must also have been in doubt. Otherwise, why were the rabbits they caught concealed in the shed on the allotments until the following day?

They were not bad men. They lived during hard times. They went out to hunt for food, and it didn't matter too much what that food happened to be. Pigeon or partridge, mallard or moorhen, rook or rabbit, all were served at our table, often mixed together in a 'game' pie or pudding, such as only Mother could cook.

They were wise in the ways of the countryside, and they never would have starved. They taught me much of what I know today and they told me of the methods described by their fathers too. Some seemed logically sound, others far-fetched beyond all reason, but, apart from those that were unbelievably cruel, I think I've tried them all. And during those early postwar years when I saw my wife and my fast-growing child enjoying the good food I'd provided, I was glad I'd paid attention.

It is said that reformed poachers make the finest keepers and, although I am deeply involved in conservation today, I could never be classified under the heading of 'poacher-turned-keeper'. I am not knowledgeable enough to become a modern keeper, but I suppose I could be termed a reformed poacher, because of my past exploits. Now that I'm fortunate enough to have my own shoots, I'm glad of those early experiences.

Often the course of learning was tough. When I was a schoolboy and a certain old 'sporting gent' used to take me ferreting, snaring, shooting or long-netting, I moved heaven and earth to make sure I was at the appointed place at the appointed hour. For one thing I knew that if I was late he would not wait. 'Time,' he would say, 'is time. Anyone who can't get up in the morning's no business thinking he can become a rabbiter.' The other reason, of course, was that his 'invitations' gave me my best chances of learning the ropes. I wanted to learn; I had a great respect for his skills and his knowledge of how rabbits and other wild life behaved at different times of the year. But I was also aware that he was only taking me to do the donkey work. To dig the holes, to carry the gear, to haul back the rabbits, to be a 'bring me, fetch me, carry me' dogsbody in fact. At least that's what I thought.

Years later I realized that there was more to it than that. I was being taught by someone who knew how to teach. I was learning the hard way by sheer practical experience and by my own mistakes.

When you have to spend half a day under a caved-in double hedge, to make all your movements belly flat, or at best on hands and knees, because standing up is impossible, when your neck and back, hands and legs, are covered in scratches, when your head is bleeding and blackthorn spikes are embedded in your rear end, you learn to dress differently and to move cautiously next time.

When you go out all night with a long net and you are expected to be quiet and not get tangled up with the string, you learn that folding down your wellie tops eliminates the flop-flop-flop noise as you walk, and you learn that jackets with buttons, belts and bootlaces are not the things to wear. You wear instead a woolly hat and a sweater.

When you *think* you can carry twenty rabbits back on the end of a pole (because the going is easy at the beginning) and the deep dent in your shoulder gets worse with every step, you make different arrangements next time out. You field dress your rabbits to make them lighter, and you string them on an old purse net which doesn't dig in like a pole or a rope.

These and a thousand others are the lessons I learned during my early apprenticeship, and I was not too long in understanding the true meaning of the word conservation.

Egg collecting today is no longer popular among schoolchildren, which is perhaps a good thing. But I wonder if we who collected eggs as kids did any serious damage? Undoubtedly we became observant as a result of our hobby and we learned to be patient. We watched nests being built, marked them, waited until the full clutch had been laid, and then took the one we needed. We interfered with nests, it's true, and in our early days, because we were anxious, we sometimes took too many eggs, but we learned valuable lessons in the process. We began to appreciate the rarer species and we never overexploited them. Watching developments often became more important than adding yet one more egg to the collection. We had all the common species anyway, we were only interested in taking those we did not have already.

A huge housing development covers my old birds'-nesting territory today, but one of the hedgerows and several willow trees still remain. It was there that a hen blackbird was killed by a marauding cat, leaving four unattended eggs in the nest. We kids took the eggs and added them to the clutch of four in another nest half a mile distant. The following day there were nine. We watched and, as far as we were able to ascertain, the parent birds reared seven youngsters. Had we not meddled in the first place, had we not learned to be compassionate, and had we not meddled yet again, there would have been at least four fewer blackbirds. We, although we did not

know it, were on our way to becoming conservationists. It was a case of replanting a form of life that would otherwise have perished, and I believe today very strongly in the practice of planting certain life forms in spots where they are non-existent – if there is a chance of their surviving.

It was natural that I should, in due course, become an angler, and my early experiences in that field made me all the more conscious of the need for conservation. I quickly understood that conservation cannot be practised in the midst of pollution and abstraction.

I once thought I was a specialist angler, but now I no longer profess to be one. I have, perhaps, become a jack of all trades. Master of none if you like, but that is how it has to be. And when I am asked about my own fishing there is no quick answer. I fish for sport and food, but there is much more to it than that.

Fishing to me means the smell of the water mint and the sound of the bird chorus at dawn on a tench lake in June; it means the rising of the mist off the water and the teetering of a white piece of peacock quill on the surface while a tench inspects the bait below it. It means the 'cloop' of a carp as it sucks in the piece of floating breadcrust under my rod tip, the heart-stopping thud as the hook goes home, the screeching protest of the reel and all hell let loose as the great beast threshes its way towards the middle of the lake in an attempt to break free.

It means the gathering of driftwood and the lighting of a smoky fire on the beach at Dungeness while the line freezes in the rod rings

and the icy wind tears its way through storm clothing and into my very bones. It means the hauling out of boats in spring, the scraping of hulls and the smell of boiling pitch; the dragging out of weed to make areas fishable, and the gathering of mussels, crayfish, slugs and worms for bait in the early season.

It means the explosion on the surface when a great pike takes my floating plug in autumn and the hiss of the line as it comes off my open spool when a similar fish takes my dead bait in winter.

It means sneaking up on a chub in the early morning and casting to it from the cover of an alder bush. It means crawling on my belly to get a fly to dimpling trout in the evening, and cursing bitterly when I make a mess of it.

It means trolling lures on special rigs at ninety or more feet for coho salmon in Lake Michigan and casting jigs and plugs to black bass in the intolerable heat of the great desert lakes of Oregon.

It means the delicate setting of a roach tackle, the trotting of a gentle glide with the bait tripping the bottom, and a keepnet full of prime half-pounders at the end of a February day.

And it means making camp in the Rockies before fishing for the tiny trout of the mountain streams. It means the thawing out of frost-covered sleeping bags in the early-morning sun, the smell of pine and spruce, wood smoke and bacon, and coffee in the clear air, little trout turning crisp and brown in the pan – and solitude.

Most of all, however, it means respect for my quarry. Hunter, shooter, fisher, rabbiter, outdoorsman, call me what you will, I am convinced that my attitude, and that of thousands like me, is the only one likely to be of benefit to our wild life in the future.

It is strange that only those of use who pursue what are emotionally referred to as 'blood sports' are able to appreciate that a middle-of-the-road attitude is the correct one to adopt. Commercial interests are prepared to exploit every source right down to the last living specimen. The 'antis' would have us leave everything to multiply out of proportion until disease becomes the only form of control. I know I am prejudiced; but I am also sure I am right.

I hope the experiences related in the following pages will go some way towards proving it.

1
Country Kids

I grew up with catapults. There was always one hanging on the big cut nail on the scullery door and several others in various stages of repair or development scattered around the rest of the house.

My father was a marksman. I never knew a better shot with a catapult either before or after his death. He was also a hunter, an excellent rifle shot and an average wing shot with a shotgun. He loved to fish for tench, roach and pike and was adept at snaring pike with a rabbit snare. I remember him once using his bootlace tied to a stick to snare a pike from the local canal! A bookbinder by trade, he turned his hand to most things that could benefit his family, even mending all our boots and shoes. He used his catapult to kill rabbits, moorhens and other small 'game' to help keep our hungry bellies full, and it's not surprising that my brothers and I became reasonable shots ourselves in due course.

Father always called it his 'cattypoult' and we kids and our friends, quite naturally, cut the word short to 'cattie'. We always had catties, and in all my years of association with the countryside, I have never heard them referred to as anything else. Catapult ammunition was always referred to as 'dabbers'. I have no idea how the name derived, but dabbers were round smooth pebbles sorted out especially for catties. The fact that we replaced them at times with ball bearings, lead shot and other missiles has never altered the name. Dabbers they remain even to this day.

When we were young, our Sunday morning winter walks started at the railway track. There we'd spend half an hour or so collecting dabbers before walking the stream on both sides looking for moorhens. How any ever remained in the vicinity I shall never

know. We gave them no peace and they were easy game for a good cattie shot. We'd watch them dive, follow their path, await their return to the surface and shoot them at that point. Somehow though, our morning hunts, which went on year after year, did not ever reduce the numbers of moorhens. The very cold winter of 1947 did more in a few weeks than we with our catties could have achieved in years. Today the stream is but a polluted ditch and there are no longer any moorhens to be hunted. . . .

My first gun was an airgun; an old but remarkably powerful tool for which I swapped a pair of roller skates. My father tested it for accuracy, pronounced it safe, reckoned it could kill a rabbit and returned it to me with a warning to be careful where I used it.

In the orchard at the back there were always too many starlings and I had shot numbers of them in the past with my catapult, before realizing that shooting big pebbles into the trees was quite dangerous. There were windows and slate-roofed buildings close by and my ammunition found the wrong mark many times. An airgun slug, I thought, would be safer, more accurate and equally silent. And so it proved to be. Concealed in the ramshackle lean-to hovel, I picked my targets and killed them cleanly. It may seem odd in these days of full and plenty, but half a dozen starlings could be turned into a tasty pie or pudding and were often used to supplement a few pennyworth of stewing beef in those days.

Starling shoots were commonplace and flocks were encouraged down on a winter's morning with buckets of hot potato peelings. The 'bait' was laid in line and those fortunate enough to own shot-

guns would lie in a ditch with their barrels pointed down the line. Within minutes the white ground would be dark with greedy, squabbling birds, and when all were settled and feeding, the first barrel would be fired. The sound of the gun going off, and the effects of a full charge of no. 8 shot, caused the starlings to rise up and attempt to depart the scene. At this point the second barrel was discharged, and the next half hour was usually spent searching out and picking up dead and injured birds. My Uncle John held the record with over fifty birds killed with the two shots.

It was not a sporting exercise; it was a pot-hunting venture pure and simple. I became adept at it a few years later when I was able to use a twelve-bore shotgun, but in the meantime I shot my share with my air rifle. None was ever wasted.

From starlings I graduated to rooks and again there was little to be said for the sporting aspect of it all. Rook shooting was always regarded as a practice that began on 13 May. The peak may have arrived a day or two either side of that date, but generally speaking the timing was very critical. Today, perhaps because our elm trees have all succumbed to a mysterious but deadly disease, nesting habits are a little different and my impression is that the rook harvest now begins as much as a week later.

We airgun enthusiasts of the past tried to ensure that we were on site during the days when the squabs were venturing out onto the outlying branches. We were not interested in those still in the nest (though farmer friends who were quite merciless blasted them out with shotguns) and we were not very enthusiastic about strong fliers. Strong fliers occupied high branches that were on the borderline of our maximum range, and we could not be sure of clean kills at that distance.

Our ploys were simple enough, however. If we could manage to be present for the whole five days (no problem when we were at school but not always easy in later years) we kept up a nonstop harassment. Two rookeries were chosen if possible, and several of us stationed ourselves strategically at both points. The object was to keep the squabs moving. By beating the tree trunks and picking off odd targets whenever possible, we forced the birds to fly from tree to tree and from rookery to rookery. When there was an appreciable distance between rookeries, the flights were almost invariably from high points to lower ones. Back and forth flew the squabs, and since they were eventually obliged to settle for long rest periods, it was easy for a concealed airgunner to take a bead on a suitable target. As the birds grew stronger daily, this continual harassment became more and more important, and the time came eventually, of course, when it was all over until the following year.

One particular exercise comes to my mind every season, even after all these years. I recall it, perhaps, because it was the first time I planned a 'grand strategy'.

I had as a companion a youngster, Chris, who was not only a good airgun shot but one who knew the value of concealment. I kept the birds moving by walking the long rookery from end to end. When possible I picked off a bird myself but mostly I caused as much disturbance as I could. It was good exercise.

Situated in the middle of the rookery, and remaining concealed all the time, my young friend picked off eleven squabs. My tally was only five, but we shared the bag, and eight rooks, I assure you, can be transformed into a magnificent pie!

Chris chose to remain concealed and pick his targets carefully. Those perched in the centre of the tree, and therefore liable to become lodged in branches on the way down, were left alone. He chose only those that settled on the outer branches. When he killed, he mentally noted the spot where his bird had fallen, and remained concealed. It was not absolutely vital to do so, but I am convinced that the silent and deadly effect of his air rifle went unnoticed. I believe he achieved more by staying put than he would have done had he raced out to pick up his quarry.

There is nothing very demanding about rook shooting with an air rifle. It requires accuracy and a certain low cunning (slightly lower than that of the adult rooks that hover in the vicinity while taking no chances themselves) but the rewards are excellent in terms of good, traditional fare. Only breasts and legs are eaten (the back parts are bitter and almost inedible) but since the birds are tender they are easy to prepare. The edible parts are removed simply by pulling them clear of the skin. Plucking is neither necessary nor advisable.

The same always applied, of course, to our starlings, though generally speaking the breasts were the only portions we removed. Apart from having them cooked at home, we kids often made a big deal out of cooking them over a wood fire in the fields where we roamed at will throughout the year. We would take out the fatty breasts, skewer them on pieces of bent wire, and 'toast' them over the red embers. The juices dripped and spluttered on the fire, as the flesh became crisp and delicious. Meanwhile, we waited for the jacket potatoes (usually filched) to cook under the ashes and fill our ever-hungry bellies. It was an adventure to us, a fantasy if you like, but I venture to say that it did us no harm and perhaps a lot of good. I recall those days when I light up my garden barbecue and cook steaks, sausages or rabbit legs and drink of the wine we have made from the countryside. I recall them too when I camp in some wild and desolate place and catch fish to practise survival. And I smile sometimes when I see my American friends pour lighter fluid onto charcoal brickettes purchased from the supermarket in order to participate in what is known as a 'cookout'. Do not misunderstand me. They are wonderful people, their cookouts are truly out of this world, and I love them all very dearly, but their black, shiny and often gas-fired barbecue units could never produce meals like those smoky fires of my schooldays. Those were the very essence of life itself.

I learned to swim in the local canal where the electricity outflow warmed the water and scores of happy kids wallowed out of their depth supported by rubber inner tubes of various kinds. When I proved to my father that I could swim (he was a very strong swimmer himself) by completing a length of the local swimming pool, he was very concerned with the manner and place of my learning. He hit the roof, but I heard him later telling my mother that she need not worry about my being close to water any more. Some years later I began swimming in the River Thame several miles from my home. It was a pretty stretch of river, clean and easy-flowing. The road to it was little more than a cinder track and there was a very steep hill halfway along it. Rabbits ran across and back to their big warrens or buries on either side and, as we raced downhill on our bicycles, we would often try to run them down.

I was off to swim one summer evening after school a little later than usual, and pedalling hard to catch my friends who had gone on ahead. In the middle of the road, halfway down the hill, a half-grown rabbit sat seemingly unconcerned and, for some inexplicable reason, I charged at it, letting out the most diabolical scream at the same time. The poor creature sat rooted to the spot, and probably terrified out of its wits. At full speed I jumped off the bike, leaving it to continue on its way while, still screaming like a demented hyena, I dived at the rabbit and grabbed it with my bare hands. My knees were grazed and my bike pedal was bent, but I had my rabbit. I had never killed one before, but I knew how to kill hens and there was little difference in the technique. I took it home later, very proud to have contributed my first rabbit to the household budget.

When the summer holidays came that year, half a dozen of us set up camp along the banks of that same river. Our tents were little more than sacking and old blanket shelters, and our beds were made from hay, straw, reeds, or anything else that was soft and available. Happy days those. It was there, and with memories of my first ever rabbit, that I began to revel in thoughts of survival. Could we not catch fish from the river? Could we not pick mushrooms and kill rabbits to provide us with much of our food? It was a thought that stayed with us all summer and even long after school had started again.

We acquired fishing rods of various kinds, we grubbed around for worms in the farmyard, and we caught eels, perch and roach. We set snares badly and occasionally managed to catch a rabbit in one of them. Mostly the snares would be knocked flat by the many young rabbits running around at that time, but when we were successful there was great rejoicing in camp. Our quarry was always cooked in a frying pan; we had no other utensil apart from the big old pot that served as kettle and teapot. Every few days we would mount up, return home for more food and a change of shirt. The latter was of no importance whatsoever, since we spent most of our time in swim suits which were known at that time as 'bathers'.

Benny, the farmer's son, became friendly with us. He was of the same age group and, although he never stayed in camp overnight, he joined us most evenings to fish and enjoy the camp fire. He had what was known as a 'garden gun'. It fired small cartridges loaded with tiny shot, and was probably designed for use against rats or birds. Cartridges cost a halfpenny each.

One evening Benny came whistling across the meadow with his gun in one hand and a fully grown rabbit in the other. He told us he had remained concealed behind the nettles on the big warren until a target had presented itself. He had killed lots of small ones before, but this time he had waited for a big one. The skin came off, the fire was lit, and the lard went into the pan. With great chunks of fresh, crusty bread and mugs of smoky tea, that creature was devoured before the body had had time to cool!

It was on that very warren where I first began to believe my father's remarks about an airgun being powerful enough to kill a rabbit. For countless hours I sat on the hill and picked off young rabbits for the camp. I took them as they came and cared little about their size. Some were tiny, some half-grown; I do not recall many adults. Sometimes, well in advance, I would block up the holes on the outer perimeter with hay, pushed in to arm's length, and wait for the rabbits to venture out towards where I lay concealed. There was a reason for these blockings, and they saved me many losses. Hit rabbits, somehow or other, even though they have been literally killed outright, often manage to scramble down a nearby hole and escape. They continue to kick long after they are dead and these death throes often took them down the hole out of reach. My blocking-up ploy proved this to me beyond doubt. I pulled many rabbits from those holes that were stone dead and never likely to move again. On the other hand, of course, I pulled out some that were wounded, and occasionally I would claim one that had been missed completely and had taken to the nearest hole in fright.

As our camp numbers increased, a local businessman, apparently impressed by the sheer enjoyment of our untamed existence down by the river, and obviously a generous man at heart, brought us down a huge marquee tent one evening. It came on a lorry and he and two of his employees erected it with our help (or hindrance). 'You might as well make use of it,' he said. 'And one of these nights it will rain and you'll be glad of it.'

It never did. As far as I remember, we had no rain at all that summer. From then on we worked at making the tent inhabitable. We dragged in our other gear and used it as extra bedding. We gathered huge amounts of dry grass and packed it down tightly in our sleeping quarters; we organized a rota system for wood gathering and other chores.

'Light up a big fire tomorrow,' said one of the ladies from the village. 'Make it long, in a trench, and let it burn down to the red embers by seven o'clock in the evening. I'll come and cook your suppers for you.'

We did not know whether to be pleased or not at this violation of our territory but, since we never had enough to eat anyway, we did as she suggested.

The fire was a deep red glow of burning coals when the lady arrived. She had with her the biggest frying pan I had ever seen, a huge basket of sausages and another of crusty bread. She cooked those sausages eighteen at a time, and we ate them in pairs, since there were nine of us. Time and time again the pan was filled with fresh fare and we ate and ate until even our ungodly appetites were satisfied. Never, we thought, had there ever been such a meal.

Never would there ever be another like it. And yet it was the fore-runner of many more. Such was the success of it all that other ladies from the village came to feed us. One brought home-baked pies, another brought home-cured bacon and fresh eggs by the score; and we did justice to them all.

On those nights when we were 'feasted', our night lines were left unbaited and untended but, for the most part, they were part of our life in camp. Food was our number one priority; we were always searching for more.

A short trip across the fields from camp was a farmhouse and yard. Scores of hens roamed the nearby field pecking and, like us, for ever seeking food. One of them strayed too far one Sunday morning, and ended up with its neck pulled. Hidden by the trees on the island, we plucked it and let the feathers drift away downstream out of sight. We cut up the head and entrails for eel baits and groundbait, and we washed the dressed-out bird in the river. It was by the fireside, resting in a bed of clean leaves, when we were approached by the farmer's wife, who inquired as to our present activities.

We were building a spit, we said, and showed her the green sticks which were to be part of it. Ernie, who was an errand boy and who had to leave early each morning, told her that his boss had pre-sented him with a chicken for our supper, and that we were figuring out the best way to cook it.

'Give it to me,' said the good lady. 'I'll take it up to the farm and cook it for you.'

It came back golden brown and surrounded by roast potatoes later that day.

At first we thought it was a great joke. Later we developed a sense of regret that we should have lied to such a charming lady. And still later we wondered (and I do to this day) whether that lady had ever been fooled at all. I have a feeling that we were not as smart as we believed ourselves to be. . . . Perhaps she knew that what we were doing was part of our growing up and becoming aware of our responsibilities. Perhaps she knew that our guilt would bother us and that we would show her great respect thereafter.

And perhaps she knew we would never do it again.

Benny had let me shoot his garden gun once or twice and I had tried the odd shot with other guns, but I always, quite naturally, wanted a shotgun of my own. I finally acquired one. It was a .410, single-barrelled, folding gun with a skeleton stock. I had no licence and no conscience and I could not wait for my first chance to shoot it.

I was fourteen and it was Boxing Day. The brook, canal and local fishing pits were all frozen, and the countryside lay silent under a blanket of deep snow. It had been a white Christmas but I had never heard of Bing Crosby.

Uncle John had promised to take me shooting that day and there had been some impatience on my part during the Christmas festivities. He was usually a very reliable person and could be expected to arrive at the appointed hour, but early rising after his traditional celebration might, I thought, prove difficult. But he did not disappoint me. Perhaps he knew how much it meant to me and what a broken promise would have done to his reputation. Uncle John was a furnaceman renowned locally for his tobacco chewing, ale consumption and sense of humour. He was also noted for his tough and horny hands. I have seen him with five young ferrets grimly hanging on to each finger by their teeth and I doubt if he felt any of them! He worked hard and played hard and his spare time revolved around his gun, fishing rods, ferrets and lurchers. Uncle John had a hammer gun. A double-barrelled monstrosity with a vague pedigree but which 'must have been worth a bit of money because it had Damascus barrels'. It fell into three different portions most times when it was fired. He also had a Belgian double hammerless which had cost £6 when new.

Dinger was joining us too, I was told; plump, red-faced, easy-going and very agile despite his build, he was at the pikel gate when we arrived. Dinger had a trusty (and rusty) old piece that was 'a good gun to kill – only it had a leak in the right barrel'. He had poked a willow stick down it to ensure that only the left barrel was ever loaded!

The farmland on the edge of the sewage works was supposedly separated by a tall wire-netting fence but there were so many gaps in it that regular footpaths had evolved over the years. In at one end, out at the other, a short cut of over a mile. It was here that we found a great variety of edible 'game', including moorhens, coots, rabbits, snipe in large numbers (does anyone bother with snipe these days – one hears so little about them?), an occasional mallard and a few pigeon. It was here too that the starling shoots developed all those years ago.

On this particular Boxing Day there was little moving at all, but I could not believe my own eyes when, quite early on, I bagged a rabbit as it dived under a fence wire. I knew that line of retreat and had positioned myself for a shot, but, although I put on an air of indifference, I knew I had been lucky.

It was about then that Dinger spotted fox tracks in the snow. 'Reynolds,' he said knowingly. And I still have no idea why countrymen in and around my birthplace refer to a fox as Reynolds. Has the word evolved from 'Reynard' I wonder?

Tracking was not my game, nor is it now (though I must confess to having developed a much greater interest in it in recent years) and I thought it was a waste of time following snow tracks but, as the local farmer had complained of being troubled by foxes recently, both the adults (wisely of course) took off on the hunt.

The trail led to a sleeper bridge, the prints went under but did not show the other side. Smoker, the lurcher, was restrained but given sufficient rope to go under the bridge so far. There was a brief snarling and snapping session, and the fox made a run for it. In deep snow it was hampered somewhat. Uncle John dropped it before it had gone ten yards.

Seconds later, and seemingly from nowhere, another fox made a run for the wire mesh fence. Somehow or other it missed the opening and, in a panic, tried to climb that eight-feet-tall obstacle. Uncle John swung on it and took it with his second barrel. It hung there spreadeagled on the wire fence and had to be pulled down, despite the fact that it had been killed instantly. I have never, before or since, seen a perfectly executed right and left at foxes! The local farmer was pleased, however, as well he might be with the lambing season due in the new year.

Dinger carried a ferret in his pocket and put it into a couple of small sets on the way back. There was nothing at home – which was only to be expected since Dinger had worked them several times before. I was used to handling and working ferrets even in those days, but Dinger was the only man I ever knew who could keep one in his pocket and have it remain quiet until needed. I have tried it many times; it would have been a convenient means of transport for much of the work I have had to tackle, but because my ferrets love attention, I have never succeeded – except with a zip-up poacher's pocket I once added to an old jacket. Open-flap pockets of the kind Dinger used simply encouraged my ferrets to try and escape. It was a never-ending battle which I invariably lost, and to this day I've never learned the secret.

We called it a day then and, with an empty game bag (Dinger had legged the rabbit and hung it over his gun barrels), I plodded back down the pikel lane. Dinger and Uncle John 'went for a quick one', which I knew would end up as several quick ones, and I hung the rabbit on my old bike and pedalled off up the long hill to home.

2
Knocker and Will

Knocker and Will were experts. Experts at ferreting, snaring, long netting, and other means of getting rabbits and other food for the table. They were not real villains, but they were not too particular about where they went to do their dark deeds at night. Knocker was an excellent trapper and spent many winter days and nights on the hills with his traps. He seemed able to ignore the elements. Cold, rain, snow, hail, sleet or high winds did not deter him. I never knew him to wear a top coat or rain suit. He seemed to wear the same old jacket, patched trousers and choker year in and year out. He had a passion for poaching and would often poach rabbits in preference to seeking them where he had permission to roam freely. Most of his profits were spent in the local.

Will was another likeable rogue but he had a wife and several children and his first thoughts were always for the family and their food. If he failed to kill a rabbit, hare or pheasant, he would cheerfully knock off a lamb or a chicken. 'Well, you can't work on bread and jam!' he used to say.

Being young and green, I craved their practical experience and jumped at the chance to join them on some of their jaunts. By day I did the fetching and carrying, much of the digging, if it was necessary, and I often put up with their continual grousing because I needed to learn. One thing I did learn about rabbiting, however, was that silence is golden. Knocker and Will could make more noise telling other people to be quiet than was being made in the first place. They did not necessarily practise what they preached. They caught their share of rabbits but I still believe they might have caught many more by following the simple rules. They succeeded despite their particular methods, rather than because of them. They were what I now call line and spade men; those who set out to go ferreting believing digging to be inevitable. From them I learned a lot, but much of it was contrary to their own doctrine. I learned because I could see what they were doing wrong and, in later years, I believe I became better at ferreting than they had been.

By night, however, they were like cats. They moved swiftly and silently. They could set a long net in next to no time and then send me off on the walk-up to drive the rabbits in. It was a long time before I was allowed to stay with the net, and only then when I had proved I could kill a rabbit in the mesh without disturbing the setting too much. There is a knack to it that is not readily acquired by everyone.

Knocker and Will showed me how to cut pegs for snares and purse nets from the covert; how to make and split the 'prickers' (twigs used to hold the wires at the correct level above ground), and how to judge the best places to deploy them. All in all they were smart operators, but I found out that they were not infallible. Even they made mistakes sometimes – as indeed we all do.

Knocker was hanging head down inside a deep ditch 'listening out' one frosty January morning while a loose ferret worked the bury. He called for absolute silence and then remained silent himself for a long time. A rattle in the ditch indicated to Will that something had moved, but Knocker did not answer his whispered questions. Realizing that he had remained silent for just that little bit too long, Will crawled along the ditch to investigate. Knocker was in a semi-dazed condition, apparently just coming round, with blood streaming from his nose. A big buck rabbit, making a hurried exit, had hit him full in the face and knocked him completely unconscious. He had a black eye and a swollen face for the next two days.

It is not unusual for a rabbit to shoot out of a hole in a vertical ditch wall, and anyone who has seen it happen will readily appreciate the power behind it. It comes out like a cork from a champagne bottle and it is not surprising that anyone on the receiving end should be knocked half silly! But the next few days were embarrassing for Knocker. How do you explain to sympathetic colleagues who know of your prowess with rabbits that you were knocked out by one of them?

I held my tongue, however. I valued my opportunities to learn too much to join in any laughter at the expense of either of those two old hands. Ferreting and long netting were still very much mysterious arts to me and, since I was never a really first class shot, I determined to make up for it in other respects. I began to appreciate the subtle points of fieldcraft and rabbit hunting; I learned how to catch rabbits by a number of other methods.

One method involved wires. Not snares, but lengths of stiff, galvanized fence wire. These were left permanently in place year after year in gate drains. Much of the time they were underwater, but that did not matter because once they had 'weathered' they became an accepted part of the drain and were not looked upon with suspicion.

During high summer, however, and particularly around harvest time, those drains were usually dry and, for some reason, rabbits liked to sit inside them. Even today you can, if you peer through a gate drain, tell at once if there is a rabbit 'at home' and if a wire is already in place it is easy to extract it. All we did in those days was cut a bushy branch of hawthorn or blackthorn, bend it to one end of the wire, then go to the other end and pull. It works just as well today and I still get a great kick out of bringing home a rabbit after a casual walk across known territory. It helps sometimes to have a partner to guard the open end while the blackthorn or hawthorn branch is being attached because, although rabbits usually sit tight while this is going on, it is not unknown for one to sneak out of the other end! A rabbit comes to no real harm from being subjected to the pull-through procedure, and if it happens to be a pregnant doe, it can be released unharmed. If there is a super-abundance, and rabbits are a problem, it can be dispatched.

I learned, through Knocker and Will, that it pays to slip a purse net into my pocket before setting out, and to set it over the open end in advance. A few purse nets take up little room anyway and there are many other occasions when it is possible to put one or two to good use on non-shooting days. You can, for instance, set one strategically in a ditch bottom before tapping the hedge down in that direction.

I learned too that some dexterity is required to grab the rabbit as it comes unwillingly to hand at the drain exit, and that it is not always easy to grab and hold it. Odd ones escaped me in my young days, and I have no doubt that others will in future, but the odd escapee today always provides a laugh. No one could really begrudge it its well-deserved freedom. In any event, there are other days, other drains, and other wires, all of which will, throughout the year, provide the odd bonus.

There is just one more aspect of drain wires which may be worth recording. Very occasionally, during an organized shoot, a hit bird, a runner, may take refuge along one of the drains. Dogs can sense it there, but cannot get to it. It is, to all intents and purposes, a lost bird, but it takes very little time to 'prime' all the drains on a small shoot and once that has been done the problem no longer exists.

Knocker and Will set off one Saturday lunchtime on an overnight snaring jaunt. They set their wires in the late afternoon and made their way to the local pub at dusk to pass away the next two or three hours before the first pick-up. That was when they saw the outlines of seven pheasants roosting in a single tree at the back of the farmyard.

Thoughts of ale left them temporarily as they worked out how to get at the pheasants swiftly and silently. No arguments about the method, of course. They'd decided at once, and quite independently, that this was a wiring job. In the right hands, an ordinary rabbit snare on the end of a long stick can be used to good effect on roosting pheasants. Will was no slouch and he knew that, given a hint of good fortune, he could reap a harvest for both of them. Pheasants aren't always stupid but they *can* be so at night, on occasions.

It took little time to pick up a wire, cut a suitable stick, and whip the two together. Then, while Knocker held the bicycles and kept watch, Will made his way cautiously past the farmhouse to the tree where the birds' outlines stood stark against the skyline. He'd almost made it when, with a great clatter of wings, seven guinea fowl took off into the night! The noise was deafening. Lights came on at the farm and a bedroom window was thrown open. But Knocker and Will had mounted up and were long gone. . . .

'When you're dropping a string, boy, let the bottom line fall loose and pull like the devil on the top.' Knocker would say those words to me over and over again and, although they irritated at the time, I still remember them well. After a number of lessons and a fair amount of practical experience under his and Will's guidance, I quickly saw the value of the advice and, although there was no longer any need for him to keep telling me, he insisted upon doing so. I suppose I should be glad he did.

'Dropping a string' means, in country parlance of course, running a long net; and while I have no doubt there are many men around who are more skilful than I at the craft, I regard long netting today as one of my most exciting pastimes.

Tales are still told of the 'good old days' when catches of ninety to a hundred rabbits were supposedly commonplace and the impression is given that one 'drop' produced that many with boring regularity; but these tales have been well and truly stretched over the years. Even in those great days before myxomatosis, twenty to twenty-five rabbits were, in my experience, the most that could be hoped for in a single drop. I recall one very memorable night when ninety-two rabbits were legged and gutted before daylight, but they were the result of no less than five drops carried out by another old netsman and me.

'Remember the night we had ninety, boy?' he would ask long after it had happened. How well I remember it! And in all the time I worked with him I never heard him speak of a more successful night.

Everything had been right. The wind was in the right quarter and the night as black as the inside of a cat, all of which would have counted for nothing had the string not been dropped and, more importantly, picked up with masterly perfection.

It is easy enough to set a long net in the dark when you know how. Picking it up, keeping the 'bagging' (the staking down of the net and adjustment of the mesh) right and repeating the performance five times is unbelievably complex. I have made two settings and, on rare occasions, three, but thereafter the net has required daylight attention before being used again.

In those early days the top and bottom lines of the long net were made from 'stay-lace', and were kept well greased with mutton fat so that the mesh slid easily between the stakes. When rabbits began to reappear in sufficient quantities after myxomatosis, I could still sense the rancid smell on my old long net when I dug it out of the shed. The mice had apparently sensed it too, however, and out of its original hundred yards only fifty remained. But those fifty yards were serviceable; a credit to the original maker.

Most nights I would go long netting with one or other of that incorrigible pair. Very rarely would I be allowed to go with them both. The reason, I suppose, was clear enough. Long netting is a two-man affair; a third person is surplus to requirements but usually means that the catch has to be split three ways instead of two. Knocker and Will had to be in a very benevolent mood to consider such a situation, but on occasions they did!

Their methods of working were the same. In those days I carried the net and ran it out at the chosen spot in the direction indicated. The bagging, as it is still called, was done by those more experienced operators. There were tricks of the trade to be learned in the process and pulling hard on the top line was probably the most important of all.

To the uninitiated it may all sound very complicated but in fact there is nothing very difficult about running a long net. Any pair of novices, after a few daytime dummy runs should be able to execute a drop in about three minutes. With more experience and improved coordination, this time could be reduced considerably, but, contrary to popular belief, speed is not of the essence when it comes to putting down a net after dark. The object is to place it between rabbits feeding well out and the bury to which they will, you hope, bolt when walked up later; and if those rabbits are scared in advance, a few extra seconds gained is not going to make the slightest difference. Stealth, silence and keeping a low profile are far more important than speed, and it is better to execute a good drop slowly than a poor one in haste.

Putting down a net in daytime for practice purposes (or for the essential straightening out after the last operation) allows full advantage to be taken of the terrain and wind direction. The net can be set to perfection in these circumstances; but by night and in earnest, it has to be set to suit the situation. This is often impossible because conditions will be found to be completely hopeless. You cannot expect to set a long net effectively unless conditions are perfect for the proposed venture, and perfect conditions mean no moon, a night as black as ink, and a fair breeze blowing. The wind direction must obviously be towards the operators and the bury being covered. If it is blowing in the opposite direction, rabbits several hundred yards away will be well warned in advance. If the breeze is from the side it is tolerable, but it tends to blow the net bagging along the lines, and cause it to accumulate in bunches at each upright stake. It reduces the chances of positive hits and makes the net difficult to pick up afterwards.

Fortunately some long hedge buries offer alternative drops. If the wind is wrong for one side of the hedge it will be right for the other and with any luck rabbits will be out on both sides. But do not be misled into thinking that chances are increased with a strong wind. They are not. For some reason, and I do not profess to know why, rabbits seldom venture far from home when the wind is high, and I cannot recall ever catching many in these conditions. A good steady breeze bags out the net nicely, allows for a good drop and if rabbits hit they are usually well and truly caught.

Given perfect conditions and a knowledge of the terrain, long netting can be great fun, but there are likely to be problems from time to time. I learned a lot the hard way, with my old tutors and by my own mistakes, and although I am still learning, I feel I have found the answers at least to some of the snags.

In order to appreciate what is involved, it is necessary to know that a 100-yard-long net comprises two lines (top and bottom) accommodating about 150 yards of mesh which slides freely along them. The top and bottom lines are joined at each end of the net through a metal ring peg which also slides freely. One or other of these pegs holds the net in loops when it is picked up. The net peels off the end when it is being set as the operator backs away from the starting point. When set, the net is held at both ends by the metal pegs which serve as guys; it is held up by smooth wooden stakes (hazel for preference) about 2ft. 6in. long every ten yards.

With 100 yards to control, it is sometimes difficult to prevent the net from bunching badly at odd points, and in the darkness it is possible to end up with a net that has most of the bagging at one end, and a stretched tennis-net effect at the other. Expert netsmen can take care of this in the setting, but in recent years I have avoided it by tying the net to the top and bottom lines with needle and thread every ten yards. It is then very easy to control each ten-yard section and distribute the bagging easily.

In any netting operation it is essential to know which is the top and which is the bottom line, and not to get them crossed. Keeping a steady pull on the top line and letting the bottom one drop loosely eliminates any possibility of their becoming crossed, and, while either line can be chosen as the top on any one occasion, I found it an advantage to mark one of them at either end with a wisp of white tape and to use that as a guide to a permanent top line.

Obviously two operators are essential. One runs the net out, keeping the top line taut, the other pushes in the upright stakes and half hitches them to the line or lines.

Ideally each stake need only be secured at the top, while the point is driven into the ground between the bottom line and the net proper. This usually allows the net to fall naturally into hollows, but very occasionally the unevenness of the ground makes it necessary to half hitch the bottom line as well to eliminate deeper gaps between it and the ground. The simplest way to drive in a stake is to place the top end in the pit of your stomach and lean on it. Attempting to push it in with the palm of the hand results in blisters before the last one is home.

Those who hunt rabbits with lamps and dogs after dark welcome wild and rainy nights, but the long netter would be advised to stay at home. There is no real pleasure in getting wet, ending up with a long net that looks like a dishcloth, and having to go to an enormous amount of trouble drying it out afterwards. Besides which it is doubtful if the rewards will be very great anyway. I do not suggest that rabbits can never be caught in heavy rain, but I am convinced that a long net cannot be operated efficiently when both you and it are soaked.

It is a temptation for the walker-up, who skirts the feeding area cautiously and returns to the net, quartering as he proceeds, to make a lot of noise to shoo the rabbits forward. There is nothing wrong with that if only one drop is proposed but if a second or third drop in neighbouring fields is considered, it pays to keep noise down to a minimum.

These things I learned when I went out on those nightly jaunts. I never had the opportunity to sit with the net and dispatch the quarry; I had to walk the fields and drive it towards whoever was waiting. After a few outings I was allowed, under strict supervision, to pick up the net after the operation was over. I was pleased, but as soon as I felt my arms begin to ache and tremble under the prolonged weight of the net, I realized that I was not being paid a compliment. I was simply doing a little more of the donkey work that either Knocker or Will had chosen to avoid. I still find it arm-aching to gather up a 100-yard net even today. As a mere lad I found it torture, and I doubt if I ever performed the task to the complete satisfaction of those who ordered me to do it. There was always something wrong.

Since then I have acquired another 100-yard-long net and have used it very successfully, I think, by today's standards. The best catch in recent years has been thirteen rabbits in a single drop, and even that number played havoc with the setting. A number of rabbits almost invariably escape either because they hit 'tight spots' or scramble beneath the bottom line when it has not been set loosely enough, but we have learned to be philosophical.

Today we use the short net for brief drops an hour or two after dark, and on the right night hope for one or two rabbits for the table. These are not deadly serious forays but plans are made in daylight with due regard to the terrain and the main bury. It is possible that better catches would result with the longer net, but these little pot-hunting ventures are not aimed at mass captures.

The net is dropped ten yards or so from the hedge bury when the rabbits are feeding well out. It takes but a few minutes to drop and, while I stay with the net, my partner Malcolm Baldwin, who is a superb worker in pitch darkness, walks well away from the net to the far end of the field and returns, quartering steadily and shaking a small tobacco tin containing a few fishing split shots. Those ten yards between the net and the rabbits' home are important. They ensure that the rabbits are still at full gallop when they hit. Rabbits slow down as they near home and a closer setting means that the chances of their sensing its presence are greatly increased. I sit, finger on the top line, waiting for the familiar bump that indicates a hit, and when it comes I move swiftly, keeping low, to break the rabbit's neck and leave it there. Trying to extricate it wastes time. It could also mean that other hits would be missed. Picking up presents no real problem and the few rabbits caught usually fall out in the process. Somehow it is easier to do it that way than to try and extract them beforehand.

Today, my part of the proceedings is obviously more exciting than that of the walker-up, but we work well together, my partner and I. We both enjoy our respective roles.

3

Nature's Apprentice

Ralph, another of my early tutors in the craft of field sports, probably taught me more about rabbits than anyone else. I owe much of my sporting 'sense' to him. He began taking me ferreting and long netting when he knew I had the basic qualifications. He occasionally took me shooting too and, by the time I had acquired my single-barrelled, fully-choked twelve-bore hammer gun, he deemed me fit to cover the opposite side of the hedge. He was an excellent shot, particularly at rabbits. His golden cocker spaniel was a fine hunting dog, but inclined to chase, and Ralph, with great accuracy, simply shot running rabbits 'off her nose'. It was not the wisest of actions and yet he never hesitated and his dog never came to grief. Nor did she seem to bother. She never stopped chasing, despite a great many 'warnings'.

Ralph could spot a rabbit in a form from a great distance. He had a natural hunter's vision in this respect and when I was still far from competent at shooting running rabbits he would often call me over and point out a particular clump of grass or thistle.

'Think you could hit that?' he would ask. And when I replied that I could, he told me to go ahead and do so.

'There's a rabbit sat there,' he would say. 'And if you shoot straight you've got your supper.'

I could seldom see the rabbit myself but I never knew him to be wrong. It was not the most sporting of shots but then, in those days, we were not particularly out for sporting shots. We were always much more interested in pot shots – in the truest sense of the word.

Ralph was the only person I ever saw catch two fully grown rabbits in his bare hands. I was used to seeing him suddenly make a dive to the left or right after laying down his gun quietly, and I knew at once that he had seen a squatting rabbit. 'Don't look straight at them,' he would say. 'Walk by as if you haven't noticed and then make your move.'

I became adept at hitting rabbits in forms with the stick I usually carried when not armed with my gun and on a few occasions I managed, by *not* looking, to dive and grab a live rabbit from a form.

On this particular occasion he dived and grabbed to his left, sprang like a panther to his right and stood up, to my utter disbelief, with a live, fully grown rabbit kicking in each hand! Before I could help him he had held one between his knees, still kicking, while he dispatched the other. By the time I reached him they were both dead!

It was not uncommon in those early days to use up a box of cartridges in the course of a morning's rabbit hunt and, although they were probably paid for in terms of food (we ate our share and traded the rest for other meat from a local butcher), we used many ruses to conserve our ammunition.

At harvest time, when old-fashioned binders chugged slowly around fields of cereal in ever-decreasing circles, rabbits, sometimes by the hundred, would be herded into the last few square yards of standing corn. Guns were placed strategically between the crop and the nearest rabbit warren or warrens, and when the rabbits broke for cover, they were shot (or missed) by the shooters nearest to them. A maximum of four guns were employed, mainly for safety's sake, but more often than not only two were needed. It was generally known which way the quarry would bolt and guns were deployed accordingly, but there were always many escapees!

When we were under-gunned, we would sometimes run a long net across the most likely escape route and trap those either missed or out of range. Sometimes our long net accounted for more rabbits than our guns and I recall a number of occasions when we used no more than a few old pieces of sacking and a bundle of hay to catch our harvest rabbits. All we had to do was block up the escape holes to arm's length with hay or sacking and let the quarry run. Nearby gate drains were treated in similar fashion and it was not unusual for us to pull out several rabbits after the field was clear. A variation on the same theme was to set purse nets over holes and drain

entrances and enmesh the rabbits as they entered. It took very little time to set the nets and they were easily carried in a couple of spare pockets.

Today, long after myxomatosis struck in the 1950s, rabbits are back in almost the same kind of numbers but, for some reason, the harvest fields have produced very few in recent years. It is possible that crop sprays now kill off the low-growing greenery on which those early rabbits fed, but whatever the reason may be, fields of ripe corn are no longer harbours for the English coney.

It was our custom in winter in some situations to work a hedgerow with the dog from one end and to place a 'stop gun' at the other. In the event that a rabbit ran out of range of the hunter, the chances were that it would run directly towards the stop gun at the far end. On one occasion I worked the hedgerow down with Ralph acting as stop gun several hundred yards away. Two rabbits ran on in front, obviously presenting Ralph with good opportunities to shoot, and I was surprised not to hear the sound of his gun. When I worked my way down to him, however, I saw that he had two rabbits legged and hanging on the five-barred gate.

'I put a purse net over the ditch drain,' he said. 'Only just managed to get it set again before the second one hit.'

I remembered those earlier incidents from then on and I have since caught many rabbits that way. Sometimes I have managed to employ the ruse on country walks when armed only with a stick. A purse net stretched across a ditch or drain will often account for the odd rabbit if the hedge is tapped or beaten with the stick to force rabbits out of cover. Their line of retreat is almost invariably along the ditch bottom to where the net lies in readiness.

Our conservation of cartridges took other forms as well, and in those days we saw no harm in lining up pot shots so that the odds were on two kills rather than just one. With rabbits as thick on the ground as they were then, Ralph and I were very choosy about how and when we squeezed the trigger. The advice never to shoot at one if you could shoot at a bunch made sound sense to us and we applied it all the time. We would sit, around August time, on top of the big hill warren and wait. Small rabbits were the first to show and they would be followed by bigger ones. It is still much the same today except that there are, perhaps, slightly fewer rabbits. We waited our chance, tried to avoid killing the small ones, and hoped to get one big one along with a half-grown fryer. We sat quite close and we could usually tell the big does from the rest, and we tried not to kill those. But if things went well we could often bunch several together by sucking on a finger and 'squawking'. The sound, very much like a scared rabbit, sometimes had the effect of making several rabbits move towards each other. A slightly higher pitched squeak would have the effect of making a squatting rabbit sit up and listen. It then presented a better target, especially when partly concealed among the nettles on a big warren. Occasionally a big buck, no doubt thinking he was missing something good, would emerge from one of the holes to investigate. Usually it was his undoing. We never hesitated to kill big bucks and, if we could line up one with another of takable size, we were pleased.

Ralph was a stickler for his own kind of conservation. Probably it had more to do with conserving cartridges than wild life but I was told by him never to shoot rabbits smaller than half grown. He had charge of the shooting; I was just a tagger-on, learning and being grateful for the opportunity. I was never allowed on the shoot alone; he always made a great thing about the privacy and exclusiveness of it all and I had to abide by his ruling.

There came a time, however, when he was too ill to shoot. Confined to bed, and thoroughly irritated with the doctor who had ordered him there, he summoned me one summer evening and authorized me to go and shoot a rabbit for his wife.

'A three-parts-grown one,' he stipulated. 'No does, no tough old bucks – just a nice roaster.' And as an afterthought, 'Whatever you do, *don't* shoot no little 'uns!'

I smile about it today but it was a great privilege in those days for me to be entrusted to the task of shooting something for the master himself. I walked tall across the meadow and hoped I'd be challenged so that I could casually announce I was there with full permission of the shooting tenant. I wasn't challenged, much to my disappointment.

I settled on the big warren and, after a while, rabbits began to show but it seemed an age before I saw my chance. Then a 'three-parts-grown roaster' appeared. I lined up and squeezed. The rabbit jumped high, kicked and lay still. I rushed over to pick it up and there, in the nettles, lay five little 'runners' – all dead. I had not seen one of them, and I could hardly believe my eyes. I felt sick and ashamed – though I couldn't say why. I took them all home, of course, but I kept them hidden. They were duly eaten a day later with crisp bacon rashers and no one was ever any the wiser.

I delivered the bespoke rabbit and was duly complimented and thanked. 'Did you get yourself one too?' asked the invalid. 'No,' I replied, 'you never said I could.' I think he was impressed by that. He laughs at the story now. He is still a close friend.

Smithy was much older than my old tutor but he joined us on occasions. He was a retired police inspector who loved to shoot and fish. Strong despite his years, he was perhaps the best 'belly stalker' I ever knew. He had no true sporting principles but was purely and simply a pot hunter. He too was a great believer in cartridge conservation, and he practised what he preached. Wing shooting meant nothing' to him – he liked to make every cartridge count. Every shooting man has heard the classic tale of the running pheasant and the conversation involved.

No. 1 gun: 'You're not going to shoot it running are you?'

No. 2 gun: ' Course not, you silly ass, I'm waiting for it to stop.'

Smithy was the original no. 2, I swear it. He would shoot pheasants on the ground, and he would wait for them to stop moving. He would also line up a pair if given the chance.

Shooting over pigeon decoys one day Smithy scraped up enough freshly planted field beans to lay out in a long line in front of the hide. I was forbidden to shoot until the birds had landed. When they were lying nice and thick along the row of beans, Smithy loosed off and picked up seven with one shot.

Pigeon shooting in those days, of course, was an exercise in meat production. Only when it was impossible to shoot sitters were wing shots ever practised. Cartridges had to be made to count if possible. Which is why, when we built a hide, it was one which completely concealed us. It had to be built near to a tall tree, preferably a dead one, and the only observation holes were those overlooking the decoys and those on the side near the tree. The object was simple enough. Attract the pigeon to the decoys, let them settle in the tree, then shoot them out. It had to be organized correctly and Ralph knew how to organize.

'You take left, I'll take right,' he would say. 'Now then; when they come in, get onto the easiest one and hold your fire. I shall say "Are you ready?" You'll say "Yes" and I shall say "Fire". That way we'll always get two down together.'

It sounds a grim business now, but it worked. And it was the only way possible to get off two sitting shots in the circumstances.

Sometimes he would hold up the proceedings while he angled round to put two in line. No mean achievement when the gun movement was restricted to one small hole less than six inches across.

Ralph had a very grand wooden pigeon decoy. Using it as a pattern he copied and carved another from a piece of deal. It took a long time, and when painted it looked very real. It was our practice in those days to use those two for 'starters' and to substitute dead pigeon as and when they were shot.

We sat in the hide one day, Ralph and I, waiting for pigeon that didn't come. Smithy had arranged to join us later as he could only catch a later bus. We had forgotten about him completely until a gunshot startled us and the wooden decoys jumped.

It says a lot for Ralph's decoys (or nothing at all for Smithy's eyesight) that they were mistaken for the real thing. And Smithy, being one of the best belly-on-the-ground stalkers I ever knew, had sneaked up on them, lined them up and blasted them both with no. 5 shot. Ralph never forgave him even though those two decoys are still put to occasional use today.

At certain times of the year we followed the hunt. Not for the thrill of the chase or the sight of the hounds, but as an excuse to walk over land where we were not otherwise allowed. We were not looking for foxes, but suitable drops for a long net! It was easy to spot a good hedge bury, one that was obviously well used and holding plenty of rabbits, and it didn't take too much working out how to get to it on the next dark night!

It was poaching pure and simple; and being 'hunt followers' gave us many great opportunities, which we followed up and remembered for the years ahead. We were never greedy, however. We went for fun and food when times were hard. Many of those whose rabbits we poached complained bitterly that they had too many but they would never give us permission to reduce their numbers.

'I can carry all the rabbits you can catch,' said Teddy, the coalman, when we took him out to help one day. So we loaded forty-two on the long pole late in the afternoon and sent him ahead while we picked up the rest of the gear. Teddy struggled and perspired, 'stopped for a fag', swore like a fish porter and flatly refused our offer of a lift. 'No, dammit,' he said, 'a deal's a deal. I said I'd carry 'em and carry 'em I will. But this is ridiculous!'

It was a bitterly cold day but by the time we reached the road Teddy was no longer feeling the cold. It was market day as I remember and the pubs were still open. Never was a pint of ale swallowed so quickly; never was one so richly deserved.

Ralph taught me to call hares. Or I should, perhaps, say that I saw and heard him do it and simply copied him. There is nothing very difficult involved, although it looks very impressive when performed for the benefit of someone who has never seen it done.

The sound produced is a squawk, very similar to that made by a hare in trouble or during the mating process. It is made by sucking hard on a finger or the back of the hand and, with practice, I am sure anyone can achieve spectacular results. I saw Ralph's first demonstration one March day when we were on our way home from pigeon shooting. One or other of us spotted the hare a long way away and, instructing me to take cover, he began calling from behind the gate. To my astonishment the hare pricked up its ears and came running towards us. Ralph continued to call and the hare came up to within less than twenty yards of where we were concealed. It sat and looked around seemingly puzzled when Ralph stopped calling, and a second later it was dead. By today's standards it was a pretty unsporting thing to do but once again the object was purely and simply to provide meat for the table. A jack hare weighing nearly nine pounds, it fed both our families well.

March hares are mad, or so it is said, and it was during March that the calls worked best of all. Occasionally the ploy worked in February or April but as a rule that was an end to it. In recent years my experiences have been different. It seems that March is no longer the recognized mating period and that hares may breed at very odd times depending upon conditions. I have seen leverets around when the books say there should be none.

There is no closed season for hares and they may be shot legally (though not offered for sale) all year round, but for moral reasons very few are shot during the accepted breeding season.

Sometimes I feel a sense of remorse, but I doubt if my pot hunting did any real harm or put the species in danger. Lying in a wet ditch as we often did in those days, calling a hare to within range and killing it cleanly as it sat, was perhaps no less a sporting action than some of the extreme range shots I have seen taken from time to time on organized shoots. I have no idea how hares would react to that kind of shooting today, but I recall that they were never really put off by gun noise. It was possible to shoot two within minutes of each other; and on one memorable morning I had the mind-boggling experience of seeing a jack hare jump the ditch where I was concealed, and try to mount the doe I had just killed. I could easily have shot it too, but even in those days I had some sort of conscience!

For a time I became almost obsessed with my newly found skill, so much so that the taste of hare began to pall a little, but I continued to practise calling. I was pleased every time my calls were successful, even though I had no intention of shooting. I remember once enticing a group of five hares, all involved in a display of 'madness', half the length of a fifty-acre meadow. At this point the old labrador could be restrained no longer. She went to join them and, although it was probably only seconds, it seemed like several minutes before sanity took over and the group dispersed with the dog in full pursuit.

I still have fun calling hares today, and it is interesting, though somewhat confusing, to watch their reactions at different times of year. They almost invariably respond by pricking up their ears and looking round but they seldom move in really close except during the 'mad' period. There are always exceptions, however, and today I wonder if the whole picture has altered because of our changing climate.

I caught hares by other methods of course. Sometimes I would set snares, high and well clear of the ground in a obvious 'through-the-hedge' situation, but I really cannot say there was any great satisfaction involved, and I gave up the practice more years ago than I now care to remember. It was a lethal method and food for the pot was often acquired without a great deal of effort, but, though it was never intended that way, certain aspects of it could not be regarded as humane. Gate nets were often used on their own or as 'extra insurance' on our hare-shooting days. We had more than a rough idea of where the creatures would lie and of the direction they might take when flushed. We often made plans accordingly and placed one or two gate nets strategically in advance. Hares have defined routes which they take when disturbed and they will opt for the easy access through a gate if possible. Small gaps or holes through the hedgerow offer alternative routes, however, and obviously it was not possible to cover these with nets also. We discouraged the hares from taking these routes by the simple process of staking a sheet of newspaper in front of those we considered to be possible exits. We did not always succeed but, by taking opposite routes around the field, 'blanking off' the gaps en route, and meeting up at the far end, we increased our chances tremendously. It was always satisfying to see a hare heading towards a hedge exit suddenly shoot off at a tangent towards the waiting gate net. Often we would not bother to shoot when it seemed obvious that our quarry would be netted, and there were many times when we left our guns behind in order to work the nets effectively. Often a great amount of walking and scheming resulted in precisely nothing, but we once had the good fortune to catch a hare in each of our nets in the same field. The nearest net had already accounted for one and as I ran forward to unravel it, another sprang up in front of me, hitting the tightly stretched section of the net at full gallop. It literally bounced out but it hurled itself at the net again and was yet again catapulted back into the grass. Then it apparently got the message and took off for the opposite gate, where the net and my partner were both waiting to receive it!

Today I would like to try the same ploys with my shooting friends but I cannot convince them that it would be both interesting and productive. They can see no further than the end of their barrels, but who am I to say they are wrong?

The mill stream, scene of my early fishing years, was narrow and winding, overgrown in summer with bankside herbage and standing rushes. There were corners where traditional float-fishing could be practised, but we learned quite quickly that more fish could be caught by walking the banks and cautiously dropping a bait into the holes and pockets as we proceeded. It was not always easy to approach without being seen, but we were quick to learn the importance of stealth. The water was clear and although by today's standards the fish were remarkably easy to catch, they were quick to disappear when shadows were thrown across the water.

The stream was slow and meandering, full of character with fairly deep holes and runs between the wide corners. We spent hours chasing grasshoppers and daddy-longlegs to use as bait, which we learned to offer without the added weight of floats or shots attached to our tackles. The plop of a loaded tackle scared the fish; a rod poked out over the rush tops and a bait lowered on to the water and allowed to sink under its own weight did not. Many times we would lose our baits as we tried to poke them through the overhanging bushes to the hovering chub below, and it was not unusual for them to be neatly purloined from our hooks before we could react. But there was the added thrill of actually seeing the bait taken, and we quickly realized that there was much more to fishing than sitting still watching a float. It was there, among the grasshoppers and the smell of the waterside, that we learned how to apply teamwork to our fishing and to look towards the catch in terms of what *we* had caught between us rather than what we had caught individually. Partnership fishing or combined operations we called it. The object was to catch fish and not to care too much who hooked or landed them. It was a good exercise, usually involving my younger brother and me, and it stood us in good stead later when we took up trout fishing.

Our tactics were to spot for one another from opposite banks and, surprisingly, it made fishing a much more exciting venture for both of us. I could, perhaps, see a fish tucked under the far bank and in a position I could not reach. I would call to my brother Ken and he would approach with the stealth of a redskin to drop the bait in and manipulate it under my instructions. I could see what went on; he was fishing completely blind. Often the fish would be scared in the process but every now and then I would see the bait disappear and I would wait until I was sure it had been well taken before calling on him to strike. Then it depended upon luck and the tackle's holding power. Some fish were big for the water and had to be hauled out of trouble. I enjoyed playing either role, even as I do today with the trout.

Every so often we would manage to present a bait on the surface beneath the bush by winding the terminal tackle around the rod tip before pushing it through an available gap. Then we would rotate the rod so as to unwind the tackle from the tip. Here teamwork was very much essential. One would present the bait according to the other's instructions because it was often impossible to observe and wield the rod at the same time. The observer would also hold the landing net and try to put the quarry in it at the first opportunity. With a tangle of bush and briar often between him and the fish it was not always easy.

We used soft wired hooks for this purpose and tied them to sub-

stantial silk or gut lines for obvious reasons. The line itself did not
settle on the water and so it remained unnoticed. The soft hooks
allied to the strong line allowed for quite ruthless holding on; fish
that managed to escape did so by straightening the hook and not by
breaking the line. The effects of leaving a fish trailing a length of line
are just as disturbing to coarse fish as to trout and salmon. Their
distress is passed on to other fish so that they too become restless.

For roach and dace one of us would sit upstream and introduce a
few loose maggots or easily acquired brandlings; the other would sit
well downstream and watch the reactions of the fish, and the rate of
the bait's introduction. It was fairly critical. If too much feed passed
among the shoal, the fish dropped back downstream. If too little was
introduced, the fish would tend to move up too close to the angler.
The disturbance caused by hooking and landing fish at such close
quarters would soon put the shoal down, but a correct rate of introduction, at the watcher's instructions, made for pleasant fishing.

There was a magnificent crab-apple tree near to one wide corner
and a wild damson tree nearby. Every season at the appropriate
time we stripped them of almost their entire crop, keeping the

whereabouts of the damson tree secret for many years, since, having discovered it, we regarded it as our own. My mother would
make the most delicious jelly from the rosy crab-apples and somehow we never tired of it.

Bullace, blackberries and hazel nuts were all gathered from the
hedgerows, spinnies and fields in the vicinity of the mill stream, but
our favourite harvest, and the one we looked forward to every year
during June and September, was that provided by the abundance of
mushrooms – delicious, succulent, and smelling of the morning
dew. We gathered them with loving care at around 4 a.m., secreted
them in the cool shade of the long grass until we had finished
fishing, and bore them home in triumph.

As a very young boy my father had initiated me into the Sunday
morning ritual of returning with an appetite. We were usually
home by 10 a.m., after having walked and fished for about five
hours. We took something to drink but no food whatsoever. Going
out into the fields for five hours without even a sandwich was not
looked upon kindly by a small boy, but my father insisted.

'You'll enjoy your breakfast all the more when we get home,' he
would tell me. How right he was, and how magnificent were those
breakfasts of bacon, eggs and great mounds of freshly-picked
mushrooms. Those insipid, cultivated, so-called mushrooms of
today are not worthy of the name. But perhaps my generation
enjoyed too many good things and took them too much for granted.

We never gave thought to pollution or abstraction, and we
accepted our pure stream as part of our heritage. We drank from it
and swam in it. My father and uncles used to set nets across it, and
drive pike into them. Sometimes they would beat the water with
sticks, sometimes they would dive in and swim around. Occasionally their grand strategy was to stir up the mud bottom to such an
extent that fish would come gasping to the surface. They apparently
came to little harm and those not needed for the table soon
recovered.

Crayfish were plentiful. We first caught them by paddling around
in the shallows, turning over stones and grabbing at whatever
moved beneath. Later we used an old bottomless bucket or tin to
cover the stones before we overturned them; and then, still later,
we learned to catch crayfish with little drop nets. These were

fashioned from small squares of wire netting and had a string tied to each corner running to a main line. With a piece of smelly fish tied to its centre, the trap would be lowered into the water and left. Often we would use several drop nets and there were times when we recorded huge catches.

When cooked later, they turned deep red and although the edible portions were small (only the tail segments and large claws were eaten), they were regarded as delicacies by our respective families. We believed then, perhaps wrongly as it turned out, that the presence of crayfish indicated that the water was fit to drink.

I also enjoyed fishing the mill stream alone and I made many early morning visits to those parts of it known locally as 'The Meeting of the Waters', 'Oxhouse Corner', and 'Paddock Bend'. I would often be at the waterside, after a long walk, just as dawn was breaking, and I knew that the first three hours would offer the best opportunities. I would follow the course downstream, stopping here and there to fish for a while. I never really knew what the next fish would be, since the tackle and bait were not specialized, but it was an active and enjoyable style of fishing. About twice a year I would keep a brace of good perch or a small pike for the table. It never bothered me. The river was clean, the fish plentiful, and I felt that it was my right, if not my duty as a hunter. In those days I could start fishing at once and walk on slowly downstream, looking and sometimes learning as I went for miles without being challenged. My angling ability improved with the years, but the lessons I learned on the mill stream have stayed with me always.

I liked to pike fish with the first signs of autumn and yet I had an aversion to using live roach for baits. I wanted very much to be able to use spoons and artificial lures but first of all I had to learn to spin with a wooden Nottingham reel. I had seen another fisherman, older and much more experienced, spinning at Marsworth reservoir one day and I decided that this was for me too. Out of some lancewood rod sections I fashioned a spinning rod and screwed a winch fitting on to the butt. The bearings of my old Nottingham reel were so worn that the whole thing shuddered and rattled when I tried to cast, but I did a 'rebush' job with a piece of tinfoil and some oil and got it spinning freely.

Then I had to practise, practise and practise. I wonder, have you ever tried to learn to cast a spinning bait in the confines of a fifteen-yard-long back garden? It is not easy, believe me. But, with a bunch of rusty keys for a weight, I learned to master the old English side-swipe. The bottom of the garden backed on to the end wall of a big hall and I got to know every row of bricks it contained. I used it as my aiming point and I worked out that I would get the right trajectory by aiming above a certain row of bricks. Eventually I became proficient enough to aim at a certain brick. I had no idea of range, of course. I knew that I was hitting the wall fairly solidly (the brickwork still shows the scratches even today) but I went to the water knowing nothing of distance, presentation or retrieve.

I suppose other spinning enthusiasts learned to cast at the water-side, but I was very self-conscious and would not venture out until I was sure that I would not make a fool of myself. Meanwhile I made up some bar-spoons out of thin, tinned copper, cheese wire, beads and lead tubing. I could not afford a dressed silk spinning line so I treated some strong sewing thread with melted candle wax and polished it up until it peeled off the revolving drum reel without sticking. And eventually I went off on my own one cold Sunday morning to spin for pike for the first time ever.

My tackle, crude and homemade though it was, worked remarkably well. I made plenty of mistakes, it is true, but I was so pleasurably preoccuped with the business of casting and working my spoon that I never gave a thought to catching fish. I quickly got into a rhythm as I walked along the river casting across and downstream. I could feel the bar-spoon throbbing in the water and somehow I *knew* that I was doing things correctly. My only regret was that there was no one else present to see how well I was doing it! I was cock-a-hoop because I had done it all myself and I felt quite sure that I could now hold my own with the best of them. But even today I often wonder whether I would have continued along the same path if I had failed to catch my first fish. I talked about that fish for a long time afterwards. So much so that I am sure my friends were all bored to tears over the whole episode.

There had been a sudden stoppage as the water swirled halfway through one of my retrieves. I do not remember striking, but suddenly I was attached to a pike that had turned and was headed off downstream.

I had no check on my reel and I put my hand over the drum to try and slow it down. My cold fingers were hammered by the revolving handles but somehow I stopped them. The pain was intense but the pleasure was immeasurable as I cranked away at the threshing fish and got it under control. Then somehow, perhaps in my excitement more by luck than good angling, I drew it into the shallow bay below me and dragged it up the gravel beach. It was a six-pounder. Long, lean, mean and ugly, but I almost stroked it with affection!

From that early spinning success, which put me on the road to becoming reasonably proficient, I progressed to dead-bait spinning. This led to the development of some of my more modern pike-fishing rigs and tackles. I caught some big pike but I also learned to enjoy catching pike of any size. We all catch more small pike than we do big ones, but – with the right approach – they can all be fun. I can't resist, however, mentioning a *very* big one that came much later in life, as a result of my earlier experiences.

'What will you do,' said one of my friends, 'if you catch a twenty-nine-pounder this week?'

We were on the 'plane for Dublin, heading eventually for the River Erne in County Cavan where we were to spend a week pike fishing. He knew, of course, that I had a pike just under that weight mounted in a glass case above my desk, and being aware of the cost of taxidermy he wondered if I would go to the same expense and trouble again for a fish slightly bigger.

To be honest the thought had never occurred to me. As far as I was concerned a $28\frac{1}{4}$-pounder was my top weight. I couldn't hope for a bigger fish and I said so. 'But,' I said, 'if by chance I do happen to get one, I shall be faced with a real problem.'

After all, who could sit and look at a mounted twenty-eight-pounder knowing that he had caught a bigger one? Naturally a big-ger one would have to be mounted too. On the other hand, how do you convince your wife and others, to whom you have said many times that you don't like stuffed fish anyway, that you've got to go in for yet another piece of taxidermy?

Well, the problem wouldn't arise, I was sure, and so I put the matter from my mind. All week long, however, my friends (if such they be) kept reminding me of the ever-present possibility and of the problems I would face if a bigger pike came my way.

It was all great fun, but on the Thursday the joke misfired. A big pike took hold of my tiny dead roach bait as I bumped it across the fast current of the River Erne.

It pulled away slowly and doggedly. I could make no impression on it with my ten-pound line and my three friends began to offer advice and estimate its weight. Twelve pounds they said, maybe more. Later they said it could be twenty or even twenty-five pounds. I had been playing it for ten minutes at that stage and it seemed then that I was the calmest person present. The fish suddenly stripped off about forty yards of line, headed for the shallow bank near the island and leapt clear of the water. Then we *knew* it was a big one.

It took me twenty minutes in all to beat it and finally it was bundled up the bank and on to the official scales. It weighed just over thirty-two pounds and I was no longer calm!

Problems? There were none at all. Well, none except for those involved in getting it back to the hotel, packing it in a wooden coffin, getting the airline to accept it as excess baggage, convincing the Customs officer that it really *was* a dead fish and rushing it across London to the taxidermist! Those problems are over now, and even my wife has learned to accept the second glassy-eyed monster that graces the wall of my study.

4

A Soldier Sportsman

There was within me an urgent desire to travel. My life revolved around my work and my weekend activities. I had made some progress at my craft, but I could see no real future ahead. My job took more and more of my time and the economic climate in those days was such that I could not expect to earn more money despite the extra hours I was called upon to work. I had less and less leisure time in which to shoot, fish and take part in my outdoor activities, and this did not suit my temperament. I made up my mind on the spur of the moment one day to opt out. To my mother's distress, and my father's surprise, I joined what was then the Royal Tanks Corps, and for the time being my sporting activities ceased. Since the object of it all was to see some of the rest of the world I volunteered for overseas service and was in Egypt on the Libyan border when the Second World War was declared.

I spent almost five years in the Middle East, most of it on the Western Desert, and in almost all of that time I wrote very few letters home. I was not depressed but I firmly believed that I would not see England again and so I lived for each day and nothing more. Despite the hardships, I learned to appreciate the desert and never missed an opportunity to study its wild life. I was only vaguely interested and made no attempt to become an expert, but after spending so many years in those lands of sun and sand I acquired some kind of understanding of deserts. I crossed and re-crossed the territory between Cairo and Tripoli, spent time in what was then Palestine, travelled across the Sinai and saw much of the Middle East. When my unit was waiting for the war (as it was for most of the time) I spent some of my hours practising with a catapult. There was no shortage of 'dabbers' on the Western Desert and I never lost my earlier form.

In certain parts of the Libyan desert there were jack rabbits to be hunted. They were experts at camouflage and very difficult to spot while they squatted in what we referred to as the camel grass. Many times I almost kicked one up before spotting it and, although I let fly often enough, I was never good enough to hit a running jack rabbit with a stone from a catapult.

My Western Desert weapon was made from a pair of pliers which, though rather heavy, made a surprisingly good prong. My elastic came from a heavy duty lorry inner tube which I cut into strips. It was by far the most powerful catapult I ever used and there came a day when I spotted a jack rabbit in its desert form before it spotted me. Or at any rate before it decided to run.

Following the advice of the old hands who had taught me, I walked on slowly past, not looking directly at it. As I drew level, I swung round and let fly without taking aim. It was an instinctive shot of the kind that is very necessary in that style of hunting. I can no longer shoot like it today, but then I only needed one chance. The jack rabbit died instantly and I took it back to the crew in triumph.

For months we had lived on bully beef rations. With dried beans, and occasionally peas, we would concoct a bully beef stew almost every night, and although it took a long time to cook, we six regarded it as time well spent. Fortunately onions were easily

acquired and an abundance came up every few days on the 'chuck wagon'. We also had an incredible supply of Italian tomato purée at the time and savoured our stews with that. We tipped in broken

hard-tack biscuits to thicken them and in the cold air of the desert night we sat and spooned up our humble fare.

The night we ate the rabbit was one we remembered for long afterwards. I had an old guitar, the top E string of which was a piece of unravelled wire cable and upon which I could pick a few chords. That night I composed a song called 'Bully Beef Stew' (which later became my army party piece) and we sang in glorious (or ghastly) harmony while we drank our beer ration. Only the camp fire was missing.

After one engagement I acquired an Italian rifle that was very accurate (few of them were) and, despite all the army regulations against looting, I kept it. It had been well cared for. The action was oiled and precise. Most of the wood construction had been removed from the barrel and only a small section of it remained, shaped like a shotgun forend. The whole weapon was light and sweet to handle – a sure thing, I thought, should a gazelle present itself as a target. But though they were not uncommon in both the Western and the Sinai Desert, none came my way. However a gunnery instructor (a much better shot than I) felled one at extreme range with my rifle and our small patrol feasted on venison for two days.

I knew nothing of shotgun ballistics in those days but, feeling the need for a 'pattern charge' to shoot at running rabbits, I made a

Verey light pistol into a shotgun of sorts. The flare portion was removed from the cartridge and replaced with a load of 'shot'. This shot had been fashioned from lead bullets of Italian origin cut up into tiny segments with a pair of pliers. Lethal!

I had no spares for practice; the first time it was fired had to be for real. I went forth one evening in search of game, with the hammer cocked and the gun at the ready. I made a wide circle from the edge of the leaguer and on the homeward stretch a rabbit started up in front of me. The monstrous weapon went off like a clap of thunder and cut a great swathe in the camel grass ahead. The rabbit was probably less scared than I was and in any event it escaped. I shelved the idea of a shot pistol there and then.

In Tobruk garrison during the siege, I fished in the sea with little success on a couple of occasions and I tried my hand at blowing fish out of the water in the lagoon. I had only some captured Italian grenades and those little red 'money boxes' exploded immediately they hit the water. Attempts to make them explode underwater caused them to fizzle out and become ineffective. The noise of the exploding grenades echoed around the rocks below and above the ledge on which I stood, and since army discipline was strict, even during the siege, I disposed of the grenades and hastened off before any investigation could begin.

Once during a rest period I caught some fish from a rocky cove at Sidi Bishr near Alexandria. With a borrowed cane pole, I joined a friendly Arab who provided me with some strange-looking beetles for bait. I did not keep any of the fish but handed them over as I caught them. They had a sharp spine somewhere in their fins that injected some kind of poison into anyone careless enough to handle them wrongly – which my Arab friend apparently did. He suffered severe pain and cramp for several minutes afterwards. I enjoyed the fishing tremendously, but I had no stomach for the fish themselves after seeing what they could do!

Those five years were the leanest of my sporting life and when I returned to England to prepare for the Second Front, I tried to make up for lost time. It was very much the close season for almost every activity, however, and though I was sent home on leave for a month, I could do little other than shoot pigeon and rabbit.

Up in Westmorland, where I was stationed for a time, I met up with an old and very wise countryman who allowed me to help with his nets and traps occasionally. (I had no heart for gin traps and I was glad when they were outlawed some years later, but I could never fault their efficiency.) He also gave me some tips on fishing, and without even considering the fact that I was blatantly poaching, or what the consequence might be if caught, I once hauled two small salmon out of the River Eden. I took one to the old country-man, since he had told me how to go about catching them. My unit was stationed on an estate through which the river ran and I was obviously in the better position to play the poacher.

Just before I was sent to France I married. I had been writing to Carrie for five years as a penfriend, introduced by a comrade in Egypt in 1939 via his girlfriend. We met for the first time in May 1944 and were married in June that year. My stay in France was brief. I returned to England on an old Dakota to Worcester Royal Infirmary and never saw active service again.

By sheer chance, I was eventually posted to Lancaster, about eighteen miles from Fleetwood, where my wife had lived all her life. I acquired a wreck of a bicycle and pedalled the eighteen miles each way as often as possible. My journey took me across Pilling Sands to Knott End where I paid the princely sum of threepence to cross to Fleetwood on the ferry boat.

Labouring along the coast road one Saturday afternoon, I was overtaken by another soldier wearing the same uniform. He was married and his wife lived in Fleetwood. He had a twelve-bore gun strapped to his crossbar, he was interested in fishing, he had been a wildfowler for many years, and had some experience of ferrets. He carried his gun, he said, because there was always a chance of shoot-ing a duck, a curlew or even a goose on the early morning return journey. Like me he had no sleeping-out pass, and had to be back in camp by reveille in order not to be regarded as absent without leave.

Tommy and I were obviously two of a kind and we planned great things together during our leisure hours. My sporting life began again from that day forth.

In those days of cartridge shortage and plentiful game, it was essential to go to all kinds of lengths to acquire ammunition. Any-thing was acceptable and it was not at all unusual for us to shoot

rabbits with B.B. loads and Verey light anti-aircraft training cartridges. Tommy and I also acquired a hand loader, some measuring
cups, half a dozen mixed packets of powder and a cocoa-tinful of
shot, and set ourselves up in the business of producing long-range
cartridges. Much of the time, however, we had to stand by helpless
while great flights of duck crossed the Lune marshes, and it was
frustrating. Between us we had Tommy's single-barrelled, fully-
choked twelve-bore of doubtful ancestry and by taking turns to
shoot we somehow or other usually managed to bring back something for the pot.

Those little bits of machinery with their table clamps and loose
handles made all the difference to our shooting hours and, strangely
enough, we achieved some success with our home loads. How we
did it without killing ourselves I will never know. The chances we
took, allied to our complete ignorance of powder/shot ratios, must
have laid us wide open; and yet we were oblivious to the danger.
Proof marks meant nothing and, like many more of our kind, we
somehow imagined that the way to increase range was to put in a bit
more powder. In fairness, we had been more used to automatic
rifles, revolvers and machine guns than to shotguns for the past six
years, and I personally had crammed all kinds of powder and shot
down looted rifle barrels in attempts to make them into shotguns.

We loaded three-inch cases and forced them into the 2¾in.
chambered gun without knowing what we were doing. Here and
there we picked up old powder. Some was creamy and fluffy, some
orange-coloured and of the same texture. I believe it was called
'sporting ballastite'. We had black powder, 'smokeless diamond'
and goodness knows what else in the powder line and, because we
were naive, we mixed it all up together in a great tin. We did the
same with the shot, which meant that our cartridges were loaded
with a mixture of anything from dust to B.B. shot. We listened to
the old weather-beaten fowlers who told us to pour melted candle
grease into the shot after we had loaded our cartridges. That, we
were told, would hold the shot together, and put yards on the range.
All highly dangerous, of course, as we were quick to learn once we
talked to the right people.

When on leave some time later, I mentioned the capers we had
been up to and my old tutors hit the roof. Rightly, I suppose. But

they too had had their problems, and without doubt were themselves guilty of using shotguns that were positively dangerous. The big old hammer gun with Damascus steel barrels was still around, for instance. That had to be cocked one hammer at a time. If you cocked both and pulled either trigger, both barrels would fire. At which point the gun would almost invariably fall into three pieces – barrels, stock and forend!

It belonged to Uncle John who was deadly serious when he preached the gospel of field safety to me. He properly made a great thing about climbing fences or crossing ditches with a loaded gun, but would cheerfully shoot all day with a weapon that kept falling apart. He could not have known the danger and, never having read anything about shotguns in his life, there was no way he could have learned – except, perhaps, the hard way had it happened.

Fortunately the gun was made safe at great expense by a reputable gunsmith at the insistence of Uncle John's son, my cousin. He could have bought another gun for what he paid in repairs, but guns were hard to come by in those days immediately after the war and there was also a great deal of sentiment involved. The gun had to be 'tightened' regularly by strips of folded foil (from cigarette packets) which were laid around the crosspin. After a time it wore and powdered away, and the repair had to be made again – sometimes in the field. But, whatever its faults, that 32in.-barrelled monstrosity was deadly in those gnarled old hands. I used it when on leave at every opportunity because I had no gun of my own and I longed to take one back to Lancashire so that Tommy and I would be equally armed.

One finally came my way when an old Lancashire poacher told me he'd 'gitten an old single barril in t' shed'. We did a deal there and then and the gun changed hands unseen for certain commodities that were plentiful in army camps but strictly rationed for civilians! It turned out, however, to be a muzzle-loader of great age and barrel length. The ramrod was intact, the mechanism in working order and, after cleaning and oiling, it looked almost usable. Today, perhaps, it would have had a value. Then it was worthless to Tommy and me, unless we could get it to fire.

I remember we had some percussion caps that were made up in two separate parts including a little V-shaped piece which was referred to (I believe) as an anvil. We also had the powder and shot already described and, somehow or other, we loaded the gun up with what was obviously an excessive charge. We stood it up, tied it to a big oak tree, ran a string off from the trigger and pulled from about twenty yards' distance. The barrel stayed in one piece, the branches of the oak disintegrated, and the gun 'passed proof'.

I fired it at duck many times after that. So did Tommy. But as we could never swing it correctly we killed precisely nothing. It meant, however, that we could both go out with a loaded gun for the evening flight, and again we took it in turns to carry the muzzle-loader. It was an embarrassment at times to see the looks given us by other fowlers, but we stood it all for the sake of what we believed to be sport.

Once, when we ran out of shot, Tommy made some! He filled a jam tin lid with plaster of paris and, when it was about to set, made small indentations in it with the rounded end of a thin pencil. Then, with soldering iron and a strip of lead, he placed molten droplets into each hole. They cooled quickly and, though not quite round, they were remarkably close to it. I would not like to hazard how many charges of that nature we loosed off, but I remember well enough that it was a diabolically lethal weapon for sitting shots. Tommy and I did not encourage game to move around when we were hunting for the pot and we got to be pretty sneaky with that old piece. I wonder what happened to it? I wish I had it today in the condition it was in in 1945.

A single-barrelled hammer gun that Tommy and I acquired later still hangs on the wall of my den. Its rusty, pitted barrels will never see another cartridge and I have made sure it will never be fired again. But, like the folding, skeleton-stocked .410 which was the first gun I ever owned, it will always remind me of days and friends long since gone.

Shortly after the acquisition of a cheap double-barrelled shotgun, Tommy and I found ourselves posted to a large house on a country estate. We were part of a small detachment where discipline was far from strict and, although we were considered to be on duty seven days a week, we were able to rearrange a great deal of spare time. An unwritten agreement sprang up between officers, NCOs and men which, simply interpreted, meant 'Do your jobs well and the rest of the time is your own'.

We bought a white ferret which we housed in the shade of the old brick garden shed and we fashioned a number of rabbit snares for use around the nearby meadows and woodland. We both had fishing rods, lines, hooks and odds and ends of tackle, most of which we made ourselves. Our floats were quills from birds of all sizes, our weights were cut from strip lead, of which there was an abundance. A pheasant, hare, mallard or rabbit presented occasionally to both the Officers' Mess and Sergeants' Mess worked wonders and, within reason, our freedom knew no bounds.

We fished for roach and eels and bream during the summer months, hunted rabbits, hares and pigeon all the time, and pheasant, partridge and duck during their appropriate seasons. We found most of our game close at hand and set our snares only a few fields from home, but we travelled to the Lune estuary for our duck shooting. A long haul across fields and marshes, our chosen flight line was very much a hit-and-miss affair. Nightly, in the depth of winter, we would settle in at dusk, to await the sound of wings in the darkness. Sometimes we scored, sometimes we failed, and there were times when we killed birds we could not retrieve from the ebbing or flowing tide.

We tried to stalk geese in the early mornings and failed miserably every time. We spent countless hours in the cold and wet and at one stage we became so obsessed with the pursuit of wildfowl that we lost out on our other activities. We stuck at it week after week, both convinced that we were enjoying ourselves. On reflection it was just the frustration that kept us going.

Riding back to camp alone early one morning, I saw a great skein of geese circle and settle in a nearby field ahead of me. I slipped the gun from its clips, loaded it and crept towards the area where they had landed, keeping the tall hedgerow between them and me. The noise they made was unbelievable – the collective noun 'gaggle' was, I thought, very appropriate. Stalking geese, I knew from past experience, was something that could not be hurried, but time was not on my side and I felt obliged to take a chance. Then something or someone on the other side of the geese made the decision unnecessary: the birds were disturbed and the whole skein took off to fly low and slowly over my head. Two of their number were dead in the air at one time and I rode back to camp in triumph with a brace of 'pinks'. Suddenly geese were not important any more. Many fowlers spend their whole lives dreaming of a right and left, and here I had achieved it by an accident. I have never to this day shot, or wanted to shoot, another goose.

Tommy and I continued to pursue the teal, wigeon and mallard of the estuary – even during our leave periods. Fortunately we had understanding wives and our mixed bags of game were appreciated during those days of meat rationing. There came a time, however, when I felt that flighting (or 'fleeting' as Tommy always called it) was becoming a chore and I finally rebelled. Enough was enough and I would have no more of it. That was just before Christmas.

'I agree with you,' said Tommy. 'It's nowt but a waste of time. We'll gi'e it a miss till t' new year.' And, fool that I was, I thought he meant it.

At about 4 p.m. on Boxing Day he came round attired in wellies, balaclava, mittens and greatcoat.

'Is tha' coomin' fleeting?' he asked.

I almost managed to get out of going, but when I saw that he was as determined as ever to go there was little I could do. He had, he said, bought a box of B.B.s, and he knew just where to go to get some wigeon when they came in high. A new box of cartridges was something to celebrate in those days. Our re-loads were not noted for their reliability.

I have been out in colder conditions since. Dressed for the occasion I have not been unduly uncomfortable on forty inches of ice and in temperatures calculated to equal 30°F below zero. I have

been cold but not too cold, and certainly nowhere near as cold as I was that Boxing Day evening as we settled in to await the whistle of the wigeon wings as they crossed our line. The sky was light with white clouds, and we craned our necks to listen.

After a long time Tommy's neck stretched to the limit and then quickly shrank back into his collar, like a tortoise.

'Here they come,' he whispered as if the duck could hear.

And come they did. Wigeon by the hundred, not high as expected, but low and fast. We dropped three as the wind hurtled them on out of range. Tommy had almost certainly taken the pair. I was too excited to do more than point in the general direction and squeeze the trigger, but I would have been hard put to miss – even with B.B.s – so thick were the birds in flight.

Tommy's neck craned again and his head moved from left to right and right to left, listening. . . . Suddenly it shrank back into its shell again. 'Here they come again,' he whispered. Two more birds fell and were retrieved.

That was a lot better than we had done previously and, full of bounce, we decided to call it a night. Suddenly the cold was forgotten and an ordinary Christmas had been turned into something special.

But there was more.

As we picked our way back across the marsh, the familiar sound of wings came overhead.

'Mallard,' said Tommy. 'High up.'

I never saw them. Tommy did, and fired. I heard the sound of a bird hitting the ground above the water line and I knew that he had not made a mistake.

'I know where it landed, roughly,' he said. 'But we'll never find it t'neet.'

We looked, of course. Who wanted to rise at dawn to find a dead mallard when we had already taken care of next week's dinners? We never found it and, having no dog, it is small wonder.

But Tommy, not being a wasteful man, was determined to find his prize and, although I could not tell why, I was ready for him when he called at crack of dawn next morning. I strapped the old twelve-bore onto the bike frame and stuck a couple of cartridges in my pocket.

'You never know,' I said.

Tommy scorned my optimism. 'There'll be nowt on t'marsh now,' he said.

We parked our bikes at the farm gate and cut across the two meadows leading to the marsh. Tommy headed towards the elms on the far bank.

'It should be somewhere here,' he said. And it was. A mallard drake, fat and unruffled, obviously exactly where it had fallen the night before. I had loaded up the old gun and kept it loaded on the long walk back across the two meadows. I thought, perhaps, I might see a pigeon on the return journey, but I was not strictly prepared for the hare that Tommy kicked up to my right. B.B. shot is hardly the stuff for hares, but beggars could not be choosers and for once I made no mistake. Tommy carried the body for the rest of the way in case another target presented itself; but of course none came.

We went home later to be greeted with smiles from our wives and that night the weather changed. The winter of that year became one of special memories. The snow lay deep and crisp and even long after Christmas, and five wigeon, one mallard and a fat hare hanging frozen outside served to feed us well into the new year!

Tommy moved south shortly afterwards and although we met and fished together one more time, we lost touch completely when he emigrated to Australia.

The old night owl I met up in Lancashire around that time was a genius. I had been collecting mushrooms when I first met him, and we talked for a long time about many aspects of the outdoors. After that we met from time to time either accidentally or by appointment. I knew him, simply, as 'Watercress'. Everybody called him 'Watercress', he told me, because he made part of his living collecting and selling it. He had, he said, 'fowteen childer' (fourteen children), and he was out all night most nights throughout the year! Someone remarked at the time that with 'fowteen childer' he must have made up for lost time during the day but, be that as it may, he somehow or other managed to provide for them all.

Watercress was a rogue. A likeable and very knowledgeable dyed-in-the-wool poacher who had but one interest: survival at a reasonable level without having to 'work for a master'. The fact that he achieved this independence by working longer and harder than most men, and in conditions which no employee would ever have tolerated, probably did not register with him. Even if it had done so, it would have made no difference. His way of life was of his own choosing; no one could have changed it. Regimentation, discipline, routine, or indoor employment would have destroyed his will to live. He was incredibly tough, seemingly unaware of the cold, snow or rain, and although basically a loner, there was a sporting instinct in him which drew him towards a younger, less experienced, but equally keen pot-hunter. I think, too, that he knew he could trust me.

It did not take long to learn that he regularly spent nights on the estate where I was billeted, that he had a rough shelter in the big covert, that he knew his way in and out of the big walled garden, and that the old potting shed was one of his refuges. I knew he worked the hedgerows with a line, ferret and spade, that he used a gate net to catch hares, and that he was up to all kinds of tricks to acquire food for the pot. I had spotted him from time to time when I had been engaged in similar activities, and being equally guilty myself, had kept my distance.

My military duties would not allow me to spend all my time in the field but, once I got to know him well, it was inevitable that Watercress and I should team up on occasions. I knew his haunts; he knew mine. Contacting each other was not difficult, and sometimes we found it easier and more rewarding to work together.

I could tell a hundred tales of Watercress and his wiles, but one of the most memorable concerned a pheasant.

I had heard many times that raisins soaked in rum could be used to catch pheasants, and I was positive that those tales were not told from experience but from hearsay. Tales of how drunken pheasants could be picked up early in the morning after an orgy of feeding on alcoholic raisins made me chuckle. I did not believe it. Nor would I believe that poachers with very limited capital would have speculated either raisins or rum for the chance of picking up a drunken pheasant. When Watercress told me the same story, however, I figured there had to be some truth in it; but, again, I somehow could not imagine that old character wasting good rum.

It so happened that, by the sheerest coincidence, I had found, in the basement of the billet, several big boxes of raisins. I was told they had been left by some Australian troops and, since every Aussie camp I ever knew was knee deep in raisins, I think this was probably true.

I had sent most of them down to the cookhouse but had kept a twenty-eight pound box and was already feeding a rough corner on the edge of a small copse. My intention, obviously, was to entice pheasants to within range of my old shotgun. Pheasants were not too rare but without a hunting dog they were not easy to shoot. My feeding them down was a sneaky trick aimed at giving me the chance of a sneaky shot.

I told Watercress of my plan and was reminded of all those 'rummy' tales when he said, 'Tha' wants to soak 'em i' rum.'

The rest of the story reads like a fairy tale, but you have my word that it is true. Down in the basement where I had found the raisins were hundreds of empty bottles. They had contained spirits, sherry, beer, wine, or alcohol of some kind or other, and there were dregs in them all. It took time, but I swilled them all out with a little water and accumulated almost a quart of weak booze, into which I mixed about a cupful of golden syrup. I half-filled a screw-topped jar with raisins, topped it up with the booze, and screwed the lid down. For two days I fed down the pheasant area with raisins soaked in golden syrup and water as well as those straight from the box, but on the third day I used only those from the 'pickle' jar. They were swollen up like miniature plums and there was a delightful smell about them. I spread them around late at night and planned to be on the scene at crack of dawn, which, on reflection, was not the right strategy. As it happened, I overslept and did not arrive until after 8 a.m.

The appropriate ending to this tale would be an account of how I went around reaping a harvest of drunken pheasants but, of course, it did not work out quite that way (you didn't really think it would, did you?). The operation was not an absolute failure, however. Standing alone, plumage glistening in the weak morning sun, was a magnificent cock bird, and I watched it feeding from behind the cover of the stone wall.

It did not appear to be in any kind of bother, except that it was walking crabwise! I truly believe that, like the raisins it was devouring, that pheasant was stoned!

I went towards it and, with a great clatter of wings, it took off, low and slow, only to crash into a tall blackthorn thicket. What followed would have brought tears to the eyes of an onlooker, and it would take too long to describe it here in detail, but I finally nailed the bird. It reeked of booze, its crop was full of raisins, and it had a broken wing.

I think I caught it because my ploy worked and that the wing was broken during the chase, but I will never be really sure. And with dried fruit and spirits the price they are today, I am not likely to try to prove it one way or the other.

I told my story to Watercress next day and he winked.

'I told thee it'd work, didn't I?' he chuckled. 'Hasta gitten any more syrup left?'

'Aye, best part of a tinful still,' I told him, lapsing unintentionally into his own dialect.

'Bring it down t' garden shed tonight and we'll get a dinner apiece tomorrow wi' a bit o' luck,' he said.

'Bring a few raisins, too,' he ordered. 'I've been feeding down in t' garden, and t' pheasints 'ave found it. But raisins will be better 'n corn.'

'What's the plan then?' I asked.

Watercress winked again. 'I'll show thee 'ow to use dunce's caps,' he said.

I believed he expected me to start asking questions and that he intended keeping me in the dark, but, as it happened, I knew exactly what he meant. It was a bit of an anticlimax for him when I said I would bring the paper for the caps as well.

I knew all about dunce's caps and their supposed deadliness. I had used them unsuccessfully before – almost certainly in the wrong places. The fact that they had gone the following morning meant they had been effective; the fact that the area was devoid of quarry also meant that either the timing or the location had been wrong. That became immediately apparent when Watercress explained that he was going to work within the confines of the garden wall.

'I'll watch 'em from potting shed,' he explained. 'There's not much cover in t' garden and I'll see where they go.'

There can be very few outdoorsmen who have not heard of dunce's caps and how they work, but how many, I wonder, have actually used them? How many believe they will work; how many regard the idea as just a romantic notion? What Watercress did was not new to me, but let me explain it in detail.

First he took a piece of brown paper about the size of a foolscap sheet, folded it diagonally corner to corner and cut it into two triangles. Each triangle was then coiled into a cone, secured and trimmed. This procedure was repeated with five other sheets and a dozen cones or 'dunce's caps' resulted. Then, using a dibber from the garden shed, Watercress made a dozen holes in the ground to accommodate the cones. Each cone was baited with several raisins and the inside was smeared thickly with syrup. The immediate area was then fed down with corn and raisins.

The object of any such operation, of course, is to coax the birds into putting their beaks into the cones. In doing so their neck feathers come into contact with the syrup which sticks and holds the cone firmly in place. The cone comes clear of its hole and the bird is completely hoodwinked – in more than one sense. It is a temporary situation and, unlike some other methods, perfectly harmless, but for the time being flying is impossible.

That open but walled-in garden was an ideal setting. Watercress was no fool and he knew the two important factors that I had overlooked. The deed had to be done well clear of cover, and to be successful the operation had to be kept under surveillance from start to finish. To be completely fair I should add that these were wild birds.

Keepers were no longer employed on the estate. It had been handed over to the military and, throughout the war and early postwar years, it had been allowed to revert to nature. Which is probably why Watercress kept his blackened billy can in the potting shed and made use of the stove inside to brew his tea.

I left him at 11 p.m. It was a mild, dry night and I realized as I walked back across the paddock that he had taken this into consideration too. Frost or heavy rain would have rendered the syrup ineffective and it would all have been a waste of time.

Watercress had gone when I returned next morning, so had all signs of the food and dunce's caps. Beneath the overgrown and unkempt privet, however, a sticky-necked hen pheasant hung suspended from a piece of green garden twine. . . .

Watercress never told me exactly how many birds he caught that dawn. And I never asked.

5

'Angling in Earnest'

When I was demobilized I moved back to Aylesbury, my home town in Buckinghamshire, to start a new civilian life. My wife presented me with a baby daughter shortly afterwards and I became more and more interested in survival at a reasonable level. I worked hard at jobs I hated to provide for our needs, and spent all my spare time fishing, shooting, ferreting and snaring. We had no deep freeze units then, but I tried to even out my catches so that none was wasted. Whenever I had a surplus I did an 'offal swap' with a local butcher as I had done before the war. Offal was not rationed, but it was hard to come by and my rabbit catches helped me ring the changes.

For many years we lived on the edge of town, the end of the road, the rim of the saucer. At the bottom of the garden was a hedge and a ditch which, when negotiated, led into rough pasture and arable farm land. It was not common land, it was owned by a local farmer who never seemed to worry too much where we walked. I spoke to him about it once and he said that most of the folk who lived nearby were decent enough and knew the difference between standing grass and meadowland. He said they did not leave gates open or break down fences or leave broken bottles around, and as he 'went to school with most of 'em anyway', he didn't mind. He was not so complimentary about those who came from town, however.

My small daughter was growing up and I was glad to be able to pass on some of my knowledge to her. Sometimes we would pick blackberries or mushrooms, or crab-apples or wild damsons; and often we would walk to the stream and paddle into it to catch minnows, loach, bullheads and the occasional gudgeon. We looked for birds' nests and watched the progress of the youngsters in the spring. I never took a gun with me because I had no right to do so, but I did bring back the occasional rabbit. I could still spot a 'form' and, as I always carried a stick, a quick swipe often made dinner for three.

After work I would sit on the back step and whittle wood, look at the untended garden, promise to do something about it, and carry on whittling! All around me for 180 degrees I could see nothing but farmland and countryside. Apart from an odd barn or two there were no buildings in sight and I did, most sincerely, appreciate what I saw; but, like others who enjoyed the same kind of life, I knew that soon it would be impossible to live a country life within fifty miles of London or any other big city. It was closing in on me then and the temptation to move out was great. One of my friends did so, to a village some six or seven miles away where he thought he would have room to breathe for the rest of his life. But it closed in on him too. He moved again, this time to the Lizard point in Cornwall. 'They'll have a job to build round me here!' he said when I first looked out of his stone cottage across the ocean.

He made the decision to opt out, to leave the rat race, to become as nearly as possible self-sufficient. Today he catches fish, tends a vegetable garden, helps haul lobster pots, combs the beaches, takes in a few visitors, and generally gets along very nicely thank you. He did what I had not the courage to do and there are times when I envy him; but I believe I made the right choice as it transpired.

When myxomatosis struck in the early 1950s I made the decision to concentrate upon my fishing. Food was no longer rationed and since I was becoming increasingly interested in coarse fishing generally, I decided to try and become a master of one branch of field sports and not, as I had always been, a jack of all trades. I hung on to my nets and snares but sold my guns and bought some better quality fishing tackle.

At Wotton Lakes, along with my brother Ken and my cousin Joe, I made many fantastic catches of quality fish. I developed a number of new methods, was credited with being a knowledgeable tench angler, and eventually I put pen to paper and wrote my first article for the *Angler's News*. To my surprise and delight it was accepted, and as a result of that, some hesitant correspondence, and the launching of a new paper, *Angling Times*, I met up with Richard Walker, who became a lifelong friend. I will always be proud of the fact that I wrote my first article alone and unaided, but it was Dick who introduced me to his friends and to other journalists, and it was he who encouraged me to write more. We became almost inseparable after I introduced him to Wotton Lakes and, later, to the upper reaches of the Great Ouse which, as a result of both our writings, became famous as a chub water.

For the next few years fishing was my life. I believe I can truthfully say I tried to ensure that my wife and daughter wanted for very little in terms of worldly goods. They did, however, miss the presence of a husband and father respectively. I neglected them, not intentionally but thoughtlessly. Perhaps I was selfish, but I worked hard and looked forward to my weekends with tench, chub, roach, pike and bream. To avoid waking the household I began night fishing and my weekends became a series of Friday-to-Sunday waterside escapes. Had I not had an understanding wife who could see what it all meant to me, my marriage might have failed. As it was I became more and more determined, now that I was no longer providing game for our table, to make up for it with revenue from my writings. I believed then, as I do now, that it was essential to spend a great deal of time fishing in order to write regularly about it. I wrote my first book, *Angling in Earnest*, in 1958. It is still in print in a revised and updated form, which I believe stands the original content in good stead.

I made a host of friends, travelled to waters I had never dreamed of ever seeing, received invitations to fish for salmon and sea trout and became very much in demand for prizegivings, annual dinners and anglers' forums. My wife, despite having been neglected was, I believe, secretly proud, though she would never have admitted it. The 1950s and '60s were years of great study, joy and friendship and I am convinced that, even though the part I played was very small, angling in general benefited from our intense but nevertheless hilarious pursuit of good quality fish.

I believe I can rightfully claim to have altered the face of pike fishing generally by developing the ledgered dead bait method in 1950. After over three years of study and experiment, I wrote about it in the *Angler's News* in 1954 and today ledgering with dead baits is probably the number one pike fishing method in use. Before then it was generally believed that only live baits or baits that appeared to be alive could catch our biggest predators. Minor improvements have come about since those early days but the basic method remains the same. Some of the modern day findings are no different from those we used and experimented with over thirty years ago during our intensive study of the method, and I smile sometimes when they are put forward as new or revolutionary!

It all began when Joe Taylor, for reasons known only to himself, dropped his rod into one of the many permanent rod sets along the bank of the Warrells Lake at Wotton while he lit his cigarette. In the brief moment it took to do so, a pike picked up his bait from the bottom, and that was the start of an exciting new venture. During the next few years we worked on it until we had tested a number of points that proved the method beyond doubt.

We never had any twenty-pounders but we had many fish in the double figure bracket and it was not at all unusual to catch twenty pike in the course of a short autumn day. But there was much more to it than that. There were the fires we lit to sit around when the weather was really foul. We had one special area where we were allowed to burn refuse and brew tea for working parties and competitions during the winter. No one minded if we made use of those facilities when we were fishing 'freelance', and I can recall many times when our herring baits ended up by being impaled on pike gags and toasted over the embers.

Sometimes we would fish the night through hoping to catch carp. Other times we would sleep in deck chairs or on piles of rushes after baiting down overnight for the tench fishing next morning. What nights they were! Full of hope, excitement, frustration, mystery. Each one was different, each one held new promise but, despite the great beauty of the lake by day, there was a certain eeriness about it at night. I would never have fished there alone, and I can remember being more than a little scared even with close friends present. Close friends like Eric Bailey, a bailiff who was as keen to catch carp as we were, and who often beat us to the water on Friday nights. Out of the blackness would come his phoney Al Read accent and his sinister 'Are you glad you coom?' would never fail to scare us. I will never know how many potatoes Eric boiled up in his old copper to pre-bait for our carp fishing sessions, but I know he used to buy them by the hundredweight.

Had we caught as many pounds of carp as Eric bought potatoes, we might have made history. It never really clicked for us, but it certainly taught us how to fish at night. The summerhouse corner at the Warrells Lake was where we learned how to handle tackle and fish in the darkness. We learned the hard way, but we learned about lots of other things besides fishing. Like the night I took a great swig from a Tizer bottle and found out it was methylated spirits! In the darkness it looked like Tizer. That is something you never do twice. I spent a ghastly night with a burned-out throat before I could get to hospital for treatment next day.

I made no claim other than that I tried always to be a thinking angler and that I proved an idea beyond any doubt before declaring that it would work. I wrote, as I have always done, from sheer experience and nothing more. I would never put forward theory as fact, and for that very reason I enjoyed my fishing and caught my share of good fish. I know, too, that I helped others to do the same.

Today it is generally accepted that carp anglers sleep for part of their long vigil and that audible alarms allow them to continue fishing during brief sleep periods, but in those early postwar days this behaviour was frowned upon by many who knew nothing about the subject. Nevertheless, we were satisfied at the time that there was little to be gained from these fish-and-sleep periods. We tried to sleep by day, remain awake during the night, and use the bite alarm to relieve the strain of watching bite detectors in the dark.

These principles were so strongly held by one of the Wadhurst syndicate that during one fishing session he took benzedrine tablets to keep him awake at night and sleeping pills to put him to sleep during the day. By the end of the week he hardly knew whether it was day or night, but on his last night at the water he decided to fish and sleep. With bite alarms set, he retired to his open-fronted tent and fell into an exhausted, half-doped sleep. At around two o'clock in the morning he was awakened by a buzzing sound and, still half asleep, ran out of the tent into the general direction of his rods, straight into the water! And the mosquito in his ear kept on buzzing. . . .

To avoid similar happenings, we decided to use bells on our bite alarms. We were aware too that noises made by buzzers could be confused with other natural night sounds. But no one can be mistaken about a bell that shatters the peace of the night, and we were agreed that the heaviest of sleepers ought to be awakened in time to strike at a run.

Maurice Ingham's bell had an exceptionally piercing sound, and we all heard it often enough. When it sounded on one particular cold night, Maurice stirred in his sleeping bag. 'Somebody answer that bloody 'phone,' he groaned. Then he turned over and went back to sleep!

The Great Ouse in its upper reaches was a water that responded to a stealthy approach and thoughtful fishing. It had very few spots where traditional float fishing could be practised and, as a result, we spent a great deal of time creeping around in nettles, thistles and tall grass, stalking big chub in summer. Our tackle was simple but sound enough to haul hooked fish out of trouble, and we learned a little on each visit. The Ouse was a river for trying out the unorthodox and over the years it paid great dividends.

We rented an overgrown stretch and, having become very friendly with the farmer concerned, built a fishing hut. At least we always referred to it as that. In fact it was a well-built, well-designed cabin with running water, four bunk beds, kitchenette, bottled gas lighting, heating and cooking facilities, and a dining room. From it we planned our summer and winter fishing and we learned how to cope with the river's moods.

Anglers from many different parts of the country came to visit us and, although some managed to come to terms with the specialized fishing involved, there were many who went away disillusioned. We were accused of lying and cheating by those who simply could not adapt. They would not give in to the river and were determined to use the methods they had always found successful elsewhere. As one angler said, who did manage to adapt – the Upper Ouse sorted out the men from the boys.

But if the river was a hard taskmaster, it was a fine teacher to those who remained observant. I regard my years of fishing there as some of my most informative. It was a clear water in summer. I could learn much simply by looking, and I spent many hours there without putting a rod together. I spent more time walking and look- ing than actually fishing. Sometimes I was utterly distracted by the wildlife, but that became part of my fishing too.

I learned to find crayfish by turning over stones in the shallows and how to catch big chub by using them for baits. I learned to appreciate the finer points of ledgering and in particular touch ledgering. It is not easy to explain a sense of touch; it is instinctive and cannot be described. It is a fact that some anglers simply cannot develop the skill necessary to practise it. Modern swing and quiver tips may be claimed to be mechanically superior, though I doubt if this is so. Once mastered, touch ledgering becomes easy, though to the onlooker is appears to be little short of magic. I learned also to appreciate many different approaches to chub fishing and I recall, in particular, one very cold day in February when the margins were fringed with ice and the banks hard with frost. Altogether it was not a very pleasant day to be out at all but, as always, I tried to make the best of available time.

A week earlier the river had been in spate and a whole lot of dead reeds and rushes had been washed down together with an accumulation of other floodwater rubbish. Most of it had passed on downstream and out of the way but, just below where I was sitting, the branches of a sallow bush leaned out over the river and trailed into the water. At this point a whole raft of rubbish had been held up by the trailing branches and an area of several square yards was completely covered. The water at this point seemed to be almost dead still and, because I had seldom, if ever, caught chub in the slacks of this river, I was ledgering out well away from it, on the edge of the main current.

Somehow, I am not sure how, a loose piece of breadcrust found its way into the water and drifted down on the surface to come to rest on the edge of the raft of rubbish. I remember thinking that, if it had been summer and this had been a carp lake, I might have expected that piece of crust to disappear. I even thought, perhaps, that it might have been taken by a chub in summer, though this was not an accepted Upper Ouse chub fishing method. Chub were known to take floating crust on the Hampshire Avon (indeed we later took plenty that way from the middle reaches) but not here.

It seemed that my ideas were quite wrong, however, for out of the corner of my eye I saw the raft bulge slightly. A pair of lips appeared and there was a swirl as the crust disappeared. This, on a cold winter's day, was quite out of keeping with what I thought I knew about chub, but it did not take me long to replace that piece of crust with another holding a hook.

I was surprised to find that, despite what I thought about the water being slack at that point, there was quite a strong current pulling under the raft. Had I given the matter any thought at all, I should have realized this had to be so anyway, but seeing a seemingly stationary raft of rubbish had given me the impression of still water.

Within half an hour I had action. A chub of nearly four pounds came to the top, took my piece of crust and was soon bullied into the net. That, I thought, was that. There would be no more chub left under there now, and if there were, they would be well and truly scared.

But again I was wrong. Shortly afterwards I had another chub on another piece of floating crust from exactly the same spot. Then I began to wonder about this particular situation. Undoubtedly it was contrary to all my chub fishing doctrine and I was a little confused. I had always expected chub to prefer baits presented very close to the bottom in these conditions and, even after two surface fish, I still felt that this was basically right. This incident had at least proved to me that chub were likely to hole up under these rubbish rafts, however, and I began to search for more with a ledger tackle.

I caught another five chub from underneath the sallow bush; a remarkable catch by the standards expected of that little stretch of river. I only once remember exceeding that number and on that day, in very similar circumstances, I had eleven.

Consider, though, the lessons learned in that one day.

First, I found out that there is very often a lively current underneath some of these held-up rubbish rafts, and it has always been my experience that chub prefer water with at least a hint of lively current nearby. Secondly, I learned that chub will sometimes take floating crust in winter, and in later years I found this to be true of waters other than the Ouse. There are stretches of the Thames where chub can be induced to take floating crust almost at any time. Members of the Oxford Specimen Group have developed this style of fishing well. They spend a long time 'feeding' a stretch right under the opposite bank with loose crusts and then, when the chub begin to show, they take them on relatively fine tackle.

Thirdly, I learned of the peculiar fondness chub have for these rubbish rafts. They seem to like to have a 'roof' over their heads, and I think one of the most likely post-flood chub swims is one such as I have described. Over a mile or so of river many such 'sanctuaries' form throughout the winter and, because of my earlier Ouse experiences, I no longer ignore them.

Because of family commitments, fishing on Christmas Day just after the war was obviously out of the question, but my wife was almost as tolerant in those days as she is now. We had an agreement. I could fish all day on Boxing Day but I was expected to be around on Christmas Day, which was fair enough I suppose, though I saw it as a waste of good fishing time.

Fred Arnaud called on Christmas Eve one year and asked if I could possibly join him on Christmas morning to pick up some live baits he had stashed in two bait cans along the river. I appealed to my wife, and she agreed to let me off, provided I was back in time for lunch.

'In which case,' I said to Fred, 'we might as well take some tackle just in case the baits have died!' Strangely enough they had, and we were forced to fish for a fresh supply, a situation that afforded us no trouble in those days. In fact, that Christmas morning was just about one of the nicest mornings I have ever spent down at the old red bridge. We caught fish much too big for live baits and we had six different species in the keep net before we called it a day. 'Plenty of time,' said Fred. 'Let's have just one quick one before lunch.' And we duly pulled in at the Bugle Horn. The trouble was we met John there, and we stayed till closing time.

'Come and see my tropical fish,' said John. 'It won't take but a minute.' And I, like a fool, believed him!

It was my own fault really, but time began to mean less and less as I became more and more intrigued with the fifty aquariums of fish. I also became less responsible as my glass was filled and refilled, and I finally arrived home around tea time to find my wife almost in tears over a ruined lunch. Even then my conscience did not really bother me until late in the evening when I awoke! Then the horror of it all really struck me and I felt ashamed.

That Boxing Day I did not go fishing at all; I really had no heart for it. We do not talk about that day any more but, while I am still tempted to go fishing on Christmas Day each year, I know I will never do so. I should be thankful, I suppose, that I still have my Boxing Days!

Richard Walker's writings, and the fact that I became friends with him, stimulated my interest in carp fishing, and I looked around for waters to fish. My carp fishing was delightful but never remarkable, though I learned to experiment a great deal, and one incident serves to remind me of those days.

I waited at the end of the lane until the daytime anglers had packed up their gear and departed. I do it even today when I decide to night fish. Not because I have any secrets or dark motives, but because night fishing tends to be something rather special and entirely different from regular daytime fishing. It is not always easy to get through to the daytime fisher and convince him that there is something special about fishing at night. He thinks that night fishers are either completely mad or up to no good during those hours of darkness. He does not want to do it himself but, despite his lack of interest, he will usually stay on if he sees you coming when he is packing up to go home, and talk your ear off halfway through the night.

I do not think anyone could call me unsociable but, once I am settled in for a session of night fishing, I do not want to engage in small talk with someone whose interests are not exactly like mine. I believe carp are hard enough to catch at the best of times, and I knew very well that a couple of people standing on the bank, lighting cigarettes, picking up and putting down baskets and rod holdalls, telling me that they 'really must go' (but never going) tend to make the fish even more difficult. So, while it is always a little harder to tackle up in complete darkness than in the failing light of evening, I usually reckon it is worth it in the long run.

I groped my way round the margins to the swim I was going to fish and was assembling my rods as the rear lights of the departing cars disappeared down the lane. Now the lake was still and undisturbed. I had been baiting the swim with soaked butter beans as an experiment because of the need to establish either a new technique or to wean the carp on to a new bait. Their refusal in recent years to respond to the regular boiled potato routine had reduced catches considerably, and it was time for a change.

There are a million small rudd in the lake and they simply do not allow soft bait to stay put for any length of time. They tear them to pieces like hordes of hungry locusts. For that reason it has always been necessary to use an 'unmanageable' bait. Paste and crust, excellent in other waters, simply do not stand up to the task and, because of the doubt involved, there is a temptation to inspect the hook every few minutes. It is difficult to settle in true carp fishing style. Small potatoes stay put; rudd cannot eat them but carp soon learn to leave them alone. I had previously caught one carp on a bean, but had foolishly lost interest when I saw a bigger fish cruising round after pieces of floating crust. From then on I had spent much of my time after that one fish, though at no time did it ever show interest. I had reverted to crust baits completely by then and my best laid schemes to develop the butter bean theme had gone by the board. Now, determined not to be sidetracked, I had resolved to fish exclusively with beans and nothing else. Experiments are valueless if they are dropped halfway through, and I knew it.

It was a fair night and the water had an air of 'activity' about it that I could not really explain, but I was convinced that the carp were there and that they had discovered the beans.

A great wallowing splosh in the rush bed was followed by a bow-wave and a dark shape heading towards the bank at my feet. There was a sound like porridge going down a sink and a piece of floating crust, left by one of the daytime anglers, disappeared. So much for my determination to fish only with beans!

I searched frantically for some bread. My best intentions were forgotten in the excitement of seeing that fish. It was a big one for the water and if it was interested in breadcrust I felt that it should be offered some, until I remembered I had left the bread at home quite intentionally so that I would not be tempted in a situation such as this. I did not even have a sandwich; savoury biscuits and a flask of soup were all I had brought to sustain me through the night. It was a sickening feeling but there was no way round it, which in view of what happened was perhaps not a bad thing!

I cannot claim to have made an exceptional catch, but I did have a remarkable experience with regard to the number of bites. Because of the nature of the hookbaits (small and rather hard), I had decided not to use bite alarms or the like, but to sit tight and watch luminous 'bobbin' indicators. Rightly or wrongly I had decided that the situation demanded a quick strike when the bite came, and for this reason I had kept the reel bale-arms closed. A bite would register instantly, and somehow I could not visualize a carp running a long way with a single butter bean, or taking much line off the reel spool. I felt that by the time a hanging bobbin had slid up the rod butt it would be time to strike and that I should be ready.

I have experienced some electrifying bites at times but I have never been quite so startled as I was when my rod tried to launch itself across the lake. The bobbin hit the rod butt, the rod tip shot downwards, the handle lifted off the ground and the reel stem jammed in the rod rest, I swear, all precisely at the same instant!

I barely managed to grab the handle and hang on to prevent the lot going into the lake. A fish threshed on the surface thirty yards out, and I tried to get the rod up but failed. Luckily the clutch was set lightly, the line held, and I was able to get the fish (a mere five-pounder) into the net eventually.

That incident was followed by a series of mishaps in the form of lost fish; fish that had shed the hook very quickly. A whole trail of disasters followed and I lost several more carp before another stayed on long enough to net. It was quite remarkable. A super bait that did everything except catch carp – or so it seemed at the time.

Future carp fishing trips did little to change my views. I lost more carp on butter bean baits that season than on any other, despite the fact that the number of bites increased tremendously. By the end of two more seasons I discontinued using them altogether. I never found the answer to that particular problem but perhaps someone else will put in the time and effort needed to do so. The attractive powers of beans, if soaked until they ferment, are quite remarkable, but unfortunately attractive powers do not put fish on the bank.

I became involved in the fairly serious pursuit of good quality fish for over forty years and I was described in a number of different ways during the course of it all. I was called 'dedicated', 'over-serious' and 'too engrossed', to mention but a few, but I think the term that has applied to me more than any other is the one in which Dick Walker referred to me as 'a member of a joyous crew'. That just about fits the bill because I learned that it *is* possible to fish seriously, to enjoy it and still find time for a lot of laughs in the process. During an angling lifetime spent meeting many hundreds of anglers from all walks, it would have been impossible *not* to have accumulated a great store of funny stories, almost without exception perfectly true, but many of them difficult to appreciate without an understanding of the character involved.

You'd really have to know Frank Murgett, for instance, before you could appreciate his peculiar sense of humour.

He invited us once to fish with him at Wadhurst for carp. Joe Taylor and I took a small tent and an absolute minimum of equipment and travelled down in Frank's van. It was dark when we arrived. Other carp anglers were already installed but apparently that meant little to Frank. He simply scanned the lake with his headlights until he found a parking space and a swim. Then he made a big thing about looking up at the sky, feeling the water and testing the wind direction before declaring, 'There'll be nothing doing tonight, lads. I'll get me 'ead down in the van.'

And I thought then, 'How right you are, Murgett. There'll be nothing doing, of course. You took good care of that!'

Joe and I spent a cold, wet, miserable night in the tent, listening to Murgett's snores. And there *was* nothing doing!

Dawn came; Murgett crawled out of his van and surveyed the scene. 'Told you they'd be off,' he said. 'Tell you what, Taylor,' turning to me, 'I'll put me beams across the water and you'll have a carp in less than five minutes.'

He stood glassy-eyed staring at the lake, performing all kinds of strange hand movements, muttering weird sounds.

And as he turned away my line began to run slowly and steadily off the spool. It *was* a run and I caught the carp – a four-pounder which was a personal best at that time.

Murgett grinned and said, 'Told yer. It's me beams wot does it.'

I was glad to have been referred to as 'a member of a joyous crew', since it established the fact that I had a sense of humour. On reflection, however, I believe I often did put the catching of fish before my appreciation of other aspects of the outdoors. It is true that I always tried to be observant, and I can truthfully say that I have often been distracted from the serious business of catching fish because of the song of a bird, or a brief glimpse of a vole, but I still found it easy to become involved in technicalities to the exclusion of the more important aspects of fishing.

Today I do not spend as many nights by the waterside as I once

did, but I still remember one particular summer night spent in company with Richard Walker and the late Bill Warren. Bill had expressed the desire to catch a carp and we, being keen carp fishers at the time, were trying to ensure that he did. We were treating the matter quite seriously, as always, but on that night the nightingales were singing.

Dick and I had become used to the noises of the night and unconsciously switched them off as we watched our rods in the darkness, but Bill, who was no night fisher, talked and talked about the nightingales. 'Hark at those 'gales,' he would say in his cockney voice. 'That's real music that is.' I am ashamed to say that we had heard them many times before and had never really appreciated them because we were so intensely concerned with our fishing. To us then only the carp were important. That was wrong. Today the voice of the nightingale is surely more appreciated than the splosh of a mighty carp; just as the swallows we watched several years later were of much greater interest than the bream and tench we sought to catch.

In the light of a powerful torch we fished with float tackle. Behind us, in the shelter, a pressure lamp burned and a kettle bubbled on the stove. We had the whole lake to ourselves and our lights disturbed no one else. Thousands upon countless thousands of insects flew towards the lights and the swallows, nesting in the nearby boathouse, homed in on them. They flew down the beam for hour after hour catching insects and feeding their young. Like us they had worked all the previous day and like us they were making the most of a golden opportunity. They stayed with us the whole night through, and when daylight came and we retired defeated, they were still working. I refer to it to this day as the 'Night of the Swallows' and I believe I was privileged to be present.

That little episode, more than anything else, made me realize that there really is more to fishing than catching fish.

6

Where Fishing Is for Fun

I fished in company with my friends for every species of British
coarse fish and, because I needed material to write a regular angling
column, I travelled to waters further afield. My experiences were
recorded in my books and articles and in 1961 Charlie Bowen, prin-
cipal of a junior school in Jacksonville, Illinois, wrote to me. We
exchanged a correspondence for five years and eventually he came
to England with his wife and two youngsters. They used the fishing
cabin as their base and travelled around in a hired car to 'see the
sights'. In between times, Charlie fished with his lures and flies for
the perch and pike in the wide corners of the river. Charlie is a good
shot and a keen fisherman with a typical American outlook. Hunting and fishing are part of the American way of life and he believes
entirely in bringing home his quarry to be eaten. Slightly overweight, he is, like me, always determined to do something about it,
but probably too fond of the good things of life ever to get around to
it. A collector of fishing tackle, he describes himself as 'an old pack
rat'.

It was not surprising that he and I hit it off. Two anglers can usually get along, but it is not often that their wives can get along too.
My wife and Jean Bowen became like sisters as a result of that
two-month visit and have remained so ever since. The result was
that we went to the United States the following year by way of
Montreal, Toronto and Niagara Falls. There then began a series of
annual visits, during which I was introduced to many American
anglers, journalists, editors, manufacturers and representatives.

At first I found it hard to adapt to the American fishing scene, but I
remembered how intolerant I had been of those who refused to

adapt to special situations in England and tried hard to understand the differences in approach and attitude. It was hard going, particularly when much of the fishing was centred around resort areas and involved professional guides and powerful motor boats. I had seen nothing like it before, and I wanted no part of it at the outset. I mellowed somewhat later and when my newly made American friends began to understand my feelings I mellowed even more.

The result was that I learned to understand lure fishing for bass and walleye. I became adept at fishing jigs for bluegills and crappie. I caught trout and catfish, and my enthusiasm for carp fishing rubbed off to such an extent that many dyed-in-the-wool lure fishers joined me in bait fishing sessions. During the ten weeks of my first ever visit to the USA I learned to look upon fishing in an entirely different light.

Fishing there is part of life, part of a boy reaching adulthood, and the angler's attitude is that of a hunter. It is regarded as sportsman-like to catch fish on artificial lures but there is no suggestion that fly fishing is superior to other forms. That, unfortunately, is what some purists would have us believe in this country, and I freely admit that my American experiences have encouraged me to ridicule this attitude at every opportunity. Our fishing would be all the better if we emulated our American cousins and fished for the joy of catching fish and not to extol the virtues of method!

The sign off Highway 36 Illinois said 'Carp fishing $2 per day' and Charlie Bowen pulled on to the farm track and followed the signs to the lake. It was a small commercial 'pay lake', only three or four acres in extent, which had been built, filled and stocked the previous spring. The owner, Harry Emrick, told us that 3,600 lb. of Wisconsin carp had been introduced – including some 200 fish over twenty pounds. Times of fishing were from 8 a.m. until 8 p.m., but Harry seemed to like my English accent and told me I could fish all night if I wished. So I did!

Charlie Bowen and I arrived after the last daytime angler had left. As we were setting up our Mark IV carp rods, we were joined by Harry and his partner, who had decided to try their luck at night too. They put up little, short, stumpy, solid glass affairs with which they fished tight-line style. I was quite sure they were not going to catch anything because, as everyone knows, you just don't catch carp on tight lines.

I stuck with soft bread-paste and crust baits; Harry had a sweet yellow concoction which reeked of aniseed and which he called 'Momma's bait'. His mother, he told me, made it by the batch, kept it refrigerated, and sold it at the bait/tackle/cold drinks kiosk which she ran on the lakeside during the day.

I was just thinking, as I cast into the deep water near the dam end, what a privilege it was to be allowed to night fish at this very well stocked lake, when suddenly the whole lake became floodlit and Harry said that just because it was night there was no need to fool around in complete darkness! (I later learned that it was his policy to keep the lake floodlit at night to discourage poachers.) I groaned with dismay and wrote off any chance of catching a carp there and then, but I refrained from voicing my feelings. But how little I knew about American carp and American carp fishing methods! It didn't matter that the lake was floodlit. It didn't matter that Harry and his friend simply did *not* seem to know the need for quiet. It didn't matter that they were using rods totally unsuited to carp fishing, that their hooks were crude and much too large, or that their tight-line methods would be sure to result in lost fish in England.

Those carp didn't know the rules! They didn't know that bread paste and crust were far better carp baits than sweet and scented concoctions. They didn't know that you can't set a big hook with a toothpick rod or that they were supposed to reject the bait the moment they felt the rod tip's resistance. In fact those carp didn't play fair at all. They took Harry's aniseed baits and nearly pulled his rods in each time they took. My delicately set Mark IV outfits remained solidly in their rod rests, bale-arms open, luminous dolly indicators perfectly still. I was convinced that Harry knew the 'hot spot' and that there were no carp in my chosen swim, but he assured me that my bait was at fault. If only I would use Momma's bait, he said, I would begin to catch carp and, after Harry and his friend had caught nine and I none, I allowed myself to be convinced. It was a good job that I did. Throughout that night I fished bread on one rod and Momma's bait on the other and, although only a few feet separated the baits, I had no bites at all on the bread.

Of course things could have been different. The fish we caught ranged only between three and four pounds apiece and all of them were enthusiastic about biting. Had the lake been in complete darkness, the big fish might have fed. Had they done so they might have chosen to eat simple bread baits and it is possible, I suppose, that my orthodox carp tackle might have been a better proposition for the big fellows. I tried to convince myself of this but, if the truth be told, I didn't really succeed in doing so!

We caught, in all, thirty-three common carp and, although we did not catch any truly worthwhile fish, I have to admit that I cannot remember ever having so many carp bites in a single night. Nor do I remember a night (or even a week) when my big landing net was put to use so many times.

Ted Trueblood is a westerner. He lives in Nampa, Idaho, and does little other than hunt, shoot, fish and write magazine articles. His is a way of life many would choose if they could, but very few could claim his qualifications. He is an outdoorsman who loves the wilderness, mountains and desert areas of his homeland, and has fought like a demon to prevent their destruction by commercial interests. He shoots rabbits on the run with a rifle and is a fine flyfisher. He loves camp fires, outdoor cooking and bourbon whisky and is unbelievably knowledgeable about the wildlife of the USA.

I met Ted Trueblood in Oklahoma and, having admired his writings for many years, was delighted when he invited Charlie and me to join him on a trip out West. We would go, he said, first to Henry's Lake and then to some of the more distant mountain rivers.

I had often read about Henry's Lake in American magazines and for some strange reason I had the impression that this was a private lake belonging to a man named Henry something or other. I still believed it at the start of our memorable trip, and I thought that perhaps here we would be able to fish away from the crowd. I rather wanted to try some lake fishing, however, and in the wonderful trout country of Idaho I wanted to see how English fly patterns and English reservoir fly tackle stood up to the test. Ted said that Henry's Lake would give me that opportunity and we travelled the 500 miles to reach it in a day, and arrived in time to do some evening fishing!

Long before we arrived, of course, I had learned that Henry's Lake was one of the most famous lakes in the West. It was named after one of the old time trappers, one Alexander Henry, who had, according to history, been the first white man to discover it.

The lake itself was nearly 7000 feet up in the mountains of North Idaho, the view was breathtaking and the fishing was free. Surrounded on all sides by the Rocky Mountains, this six-mile-long expanse of blue water was magnificent and I could not wait to fish it. Strangely enough, I could see no boats and no anglers, and my first impression was that we had the whole lake to ourselves. But a shock awaited me when we reached the far side where Ted had reserved a log cabin and a boat for us. There were approximately thirty boats, each holding one, two, or three anglers, anchored off the narrow bay which formed the boat dock. Trout were leaping, twisting and turning in the bay; the water was alive with fish and a wire stretched across it bore the notice 'No fishing beyond this point'.

Ted pointed to the circle of boats and I watched the anglers. Some were casting flies, some were spinning, some were float fishing with worms but none was catching fish. 'Out there,' said Ted, 'is the Glory Hole.'

Glory Hole it surely was, and I soon learned the reason for its name. At this end of the lake, in the bay where the trout were so active, was a big spring which flowed out into the lake and cooled down the water in the twenty-feet-deep hole just off the shore. At this late stage in the season, the rest of the lake, which was shallow and weedy, was too warm for the trout to remain dispersed and they accumulated in the Glory Hole. It seemed that all the anglers had done the same thing!

I was appalled at the thought of joining this 'gold rush', and I remarked to Ted that it was small wonder no one was catching any fish. I felt sure that the noise and disturbance caused by thirty boats, thirty outboard motors, thirty rattling anchor chains and something like a hundred anglers must surely scare the daylights out of them.

'Wait and see,' said Ted. 'You may be surprised.'

We joined that milling mass of boats, Charlie, Ted and I, and we fished until it was dark. We caught nothing and saw nothing caught. And I was not at all surprised.

Before daylight next morning Ted called us to go out again. I looked across the dark water and could see the shapes of boats already in position and I groaned. What chance in such circumstances?

It was light when we reached our spot and I lowered the anchor gently so as to keep the chain from scraping the metal bows of the boat. All around us trout began to rise, roll, prime and splash, and my first thought was to put on a dry fly and fish the surface. Ted advised against it. 'These trout show on the top,' he said, 'but you never catch them there. *Always* they lie deep.'

To emphasize his point he put on a slow-sinking shooting head and began to fish, counting the seconds while his fly sank and increasing the countdown until he began to pick up weed. I followed suit and learned that, with my number eight head, I had to allow twenty-five seconds by my watch before I could retrieve at the right depth.

All around the trout kept rising. Charlie caught a two-pounder on spinning tackle and a diabolical-looking creation called an Ugly Bug jig. This was encouraging and I was tempted to change tactics, but Ted told me to stick with the fly. It was, he said, only a question of finding the right pattern.

I looked around the surface of the water. It was covered with tiny green flies and I looked for something green in my fly box. There were some tiny green nymphs which my brother Ken had tied and I attached one and skidded it across the top of the water. On about the third cast there was a boil as the nymph landed and the reel screamed as a trout tore off ten yards of line. 'What about the surface now then?' I said as I boated a three-pound cutthroat. Ted grinned and said that I had just experienced some of my usual English luck and that he would lay fifty dollars I couldn't do it again!

It's as well I didn't take him. For the rest of my stay I never saw another fish come to a surface fly. But that morning, on little brown nymphs fished slowly at about twenty feet, Ted caught three fish and I caught another two. All were three-pounders and all were cutthroats – beautiful strong fish with blood-red markings under the chin, which obviously gave them their name. We went ashore that breakfast time with seven fish. No other boat had fared as well and I was proud to have held my own with Ted.

We caught more fish from the Glory Hole during the next two days but none was bigger than our first three-pounders. We had blanks and successes but at the end of it all I found myself agreeing with the bearded old-timer there who had said of these trout, 'If they's hittin' you can catch 'em; if they ain't – you cain't!'

We left Henry's Lake soon after daybreak and journeyed through Yellowstone Park in search of a new camp site. Old Faithful, a very famous geyser, emptied especially for our benefit as we passed through and I spent much time marvelling at the hot springs, the bears and the magnificent, breathtaking beauty of that mountainous countryside. The memories of that journey will always be with me.

Before we left the lake I filleted some of the trout we had caught and we had further been presented with some smoked fillets by another angler who had a surplus. 'Momma found a new recipe for smoked fish,' he said to Ted. 'Sure would be pleased for you to try some.'

Ted accepted them graciously and we put them in the icebox with the canned beer. Later that day we ate them during one of our

roadside stops and my only regret is that we never found out just
how 'Momma' had prepared them. They were delicious.

So, too, were the cutthroat fillets we fried for supper that night
and ate by the big log fire.

From among the pile of bedding, tackle and provisions in the back
of the truck, Ted produced a bottle of Scotch whisky, and we diluted
it with the icy water of a nearby creek. It was one o'clock in the
morning before we finished yarning and crawled into our sleeping
bags. The whisky had left me a little light-headed despite the fact
that I had been very sparing with it. What I had failed to recognize
was the fact that in the rare air of the mountains its effect was considerably stronger than at lower levels. We had travelled a long way
and I was pleasantly tired, but before I went to sleep I spoke to Ted
about the next day's fishing. Where would we go; what would we
fish for? 'Wait until daylight,' said Ted, 'and I will show you the
Madison River.'

He woke me at dawn and we stood on the edge of the bluff and
looked down on the Madison hundreds of feet below. I knew there
and then that this was a river I *had* to fish! It was quite the most
remarkable-looking stretch of river I have ever seen, because at no
point did it flow straight for more than fifty yards. It wound and
twisted, doubled back on itself and formed pools, eddies and back-
waters the likes of which I have never seen anywhere else in the
world. The banks were swampy and covered with osier-type
bushes. Beavers had cut inroads into the bankside foliage and I
could see that there were deep channels and holes which would
make the going treacherous. But I understood now what Ted Trueblood had meant when he said, 'If you walk down the Madison for
half an hour it will take you a day to fish it back!' Such is the meandering course of this river that a straight walk downstream of half a
mile would mean, perhaps, a three-miles-long return journey following the bank proper.

We were 8000 feet up in the mountains of Montana and we
moved down to a level nearer the river bank to make camp about
fifty yards from the water's edge. On the way down I saw one lone
angler fishing about five miles away and I thought that, at the present rate of progress, it would take him about a week to reach us! I
felt sure we would be able to fish undisturbed and so it proved to be.

In the two days that followed I fished less than a hundred yards of bank and, in fact, I spent most of my time in two wide corners where the deep water cut in close to my own bank and formed an ideal run for long trotting. I'm quite sure that there wasn't another angler within several miles and I was further convinced that this river was hardly ever fished at this point. You can always tell where anglers have been. The bankside becomes worn and recognized swims become very obvious. My problem here was getting near enough to the water to fish and I never managed it without sinking up to my thighs in cold, black, muddy water at least once. By day it was fine; the sun soon dried me out, but in the evenings it chills off quickly and I soon learned to appreciate the warmth of the camp fire.

To the best of my knowledge there were only brown trout and whitefish in the Madison River at that point, and while I was happy to catch trout, I particularly wanted to try my hand with the whitefish. American anglers are not interested in them and, because they have small mouths, they are written off as uncatchable anyway by the majority of lure and fly fishermen.

But what a challenge for English trotting and ledgering techniques! I caught a few trout by various means but it was not long before I was looking into the crystal clear water for these so-called whitefish. And I found some in two places.

The first shoal scattered in all directions as my shadow fell on the water, and I left them strictly alone, marking the exact spot for later. I was more careful after that; as careful as ploughing my way through the swamp looking for a piece of dry bank would allow me to be. And I spotted another shoal lying deep in about ten feet of water. The only baits I had were a few lobworms. They were on the big side, but I put a whole one on to see what the form was, and I trotted it down on three-pound tackle from well upstream using a big fluted float. I had a bite almost every trot down but I failed to connect each time. How I wished I had some maggots! Trotting is a great way of catching fish and I'm quite aware that you can use baits other than maggots, but I'm sure that maggots on the hook, and fed in regularly along the same path, offer by far the greatest chance of success. I had no means of groundbaiting and I wasn't too sure of the legality of it anyway, but I ended up by using the tiniest piece of worm on a number sixteen hook and chopping the rest up for

groundbait. Then I began to catch the whitefish. I'll remember the
first one for a long time. It weighed about three pounds and in the
very fast water of the Madison, and on about a pound-and-a-half
hook link, it gave me some anxious moments.

When I finally landed it I could smell thyme and my first thought
was that these so-called whitefish were really grayling. The scaling,
shape and mouth of the fish were almost exactly like our grayling.
The fight it put up was similar too. But the dorsal fin was short and
in no wise like that of a grayling.

I don't know how many I caught but I do remember that it was
extremely pleasant fishing. I put most of them back (we had an
abundance of trout so there was no point in keeping many for food),
but I kept a couple to fry for breakfast one morning.

I wanted to try for them with ledger tackle but as I didn't have a
proper ledger rod with me I used a very soft-actioned fly rod. It
wasn't the best rod for casting a five-swan-shot ledger tackle, but it
did register the bites extraordinarily well. The soft tip set up no
immediate resistance to the fish and it moved round slowly to a full
quarter-circle with each bite.

But I had most fun on my long hollow glass roach rod. I found a
spot where I could fish for these whitefish unseen and at close
range. I was able to hold the rod and watch them take the bait in the
crystal clear water time and time again. Not surprisingly, I did not
want to leave them. I enjoyed catching them so much, but all too
soon it was time to strike camp and push on higher up into the
mountains of Wyoming and Idaho to fish the many creeks and
rivers for native cutthroats and brook trout, to stop and lunch off
bread and cheese and iced beer, to look down into the valleys and
marvel at the sheer size of it all, to construct soft and springy beds of
spruce twigs and to breathe in the soft scent of them that permeated
through our pillows and lulled us to sleep in the cold mountain air.

Then it was time to leave the mountains and begin the long
descent which would take us back to so-called civilization. We stopped here and there at leisure to view the fishing prospects and soon
we were at Picabo. Now we were on the last lap of our journey and
in the morning Charlie and I had to fly back to St. Louis. We needed
a couple of trout to take home with us.

It's not easy keeping fish fresh out there. The temperature gets up to ninety plus by day and, even with ice and cooler boxes, they soon deteriorate. In any case we'd eaten most of our fish as soon as we'd caught them. So here we were on Silver Creek, a river which, had it not been for its rather swampy banks, could have been mistaken for the Hampshire Avon. It was deep, fast, very clear and full of lush streamer weed. It held, as far as I could ascertain, just two species of fish, rainbow trout and American brook trout, both of which spawn there naturally.

There were no restrictions regarding method, but, as on all American waters, bag limits were strictly enforced. Not that I wanted a limit. What would I do with seven trout? It was about 2.30 p.m. and I had but a couple of hours in which to fish. It was not the best of times for fly fishing, but because we'd done well with fly all week, we put up fly tackle and gave it a try. Ted, a genius with a fly rod, took six fish which were just about takeable, but returned them all hoping, and confidently expecting, to take a big one eventually. Charlie could only take undersized fish and I caught but one small brook trout which I returned before anyone else saw it.

Time passed and eventually I decided that more efficient measures were called for. I put up my light ledger rod, took a box of lobworms (or, as I had by now learned to call them, nite crawlers) and baited up a three-swan-shot rig. I'd acquired those nite crawlers from a slot machine in the middle of the Idaho desert country! We came across a small filling station literally miles from anywhere and there, large as life, was a worm-dispensing machine. At fifty cents a dozen they were the most expensive worms I'd ever bought but I couldn't have bought better ones anywhere. And as I'd already been through the most depressing (to me) experience of having to fish several American waters without bait of any kind I welcomed the opportunity to purchase some fresh worms.

I rolled and scratched around the deep run below the bridge until I felt I knew every inch of it; but I had not so much as a touch and I began to despair of ever seeing my take-home trout. I knew that if I failed to produce the goods my American friends would never let me live it down, and I resigned myself to a ribbing.

It was nearly time to go and I strolled back to the road bridge where the camper truck was parked. It was a wooden structure only a few feet above the water and I studied the current carefully. It ran deep and fast. A strand of barbed wire, festooned with broken lines, was stretched across the downstream end. Obviously it was a heavily fished spot and I did not rate my chances very highly, but, as I had to wait for Ted to return, I thought I might as well do it with a bait in the water.

I flicked a lobworm under the bridge and let it roll down with the current. Nothing. Again, and again nothing. Charlie returned and stood watching me from well back; Ted was having a few final casts in the upstream meadow but was obviously still having as lean a time as I was. I tossed the worm box to Charlie and asked him to stand on the bridge above where I was sitting, break up the few remaining lobs and drop them into the water a piece at a time.

I watched several pieces go under the bridge and followed them down with my hook bait, holding the rod fairly high to keep the tackle at about the same depth as Charlie's free offerings. Suddenly the rod tip thumped round in a quarter circle and the reel clutch slipped momentarily. I woke up to the fact that I was into a fish just about in time to stop it wrapping itself round the middle pier of the bridge! Even now I don't know how that three-pound line held. There was no way of landing the fish other than by hauling it back against the current and bullying it out of the mass of debris that had collected under the bridge. It was a three-pound rainbow and it spent more time out of the water than in until I got the net under it.

Ted, who arrived at that moment, was very pleased and said he thought we ought to record the capture and the location. He took my camera and photographed the fish, then asked me to make another cast so that he could take a location shot. I flicked the worm out under the bridge again and the rod was nearly wrenched from my hand! Another rainbow! This one was smaller but at about two pounds still well worth taking. With the fish safely in the net I knew that my reputation was saved, but that last-minute reprieve was too close for my liking.

We arrived at Ted's home in Nampa where we feasted royally and spent several hours in the basement which is Ted's office, gun and tackle room, photographic dark room and general den. I rummaged through his fly-tying materials and took away furs and feathers the likes of which I could never hope to find in England and which have proved invaluable to me since. And I believe if Charlie or I had expressed a liking for the top brick of the chimney Ted would have given it to us. As it was we had to borrow an extra rucksack to take away all the extra 'goodies'. Fortunately there were no strict luggage restrictions on the plane.

Ted took us to the airport and saw us off. He was still wearing his baseball cap and his cheerful grin as he waved goodbye to us across the black tarmac. Both Charlie and I were truly sad to go.

My accounts of fishing in the USA interested several readers of *Anglers' Mail* to such an extent that they asked me to organize a trip so that they might join me in similar experiences. In due course, and after a great deal of organizing, a dozen of us took off from Heathrow heading for Beaver Lake, Arkansas.

We flew over the St. Louis area when it seemed that there was more water than land. St. Louis is referred to as the place where the 'muddy waters meet', which simply means that the Mississippi joins the Missouri at that point. On that day they were literally one; and countless thousands of acres were under water. Anglers were actually catching carp and catfish by sitting on the upper highway and fishing into the water that covered the lower road!

At Beaver there was an all-time record of high water the colour of milk chocolate but we were still able to find the odd bass, crappie and carp in the coves and protected bays. We caught fish among tree tops which a few weeks previously had been on dry land; but it was hard. Kevin Clifford and Bill Watson from Hull, Derek Frame, the Hendon tackleist, and several others caught carp up to eleven pounds while waiting patiently for the water to subside. We all knew it was not going to do so while we were there, but no one seemed to care too much. There were compensations and undoubtedly the very happy-go-lucky attitude of the American angler rubbed off a little. Fishing is for fun out there, and there was no serious, early-to-rise-stick-at-it-all-day intensity like there is in England. We rose when we felt like it, wandered down to the little restaurant on Rocky Branch, ate a leisurely breakfast, told lies for an hour or so, and then went fishing. Some went for carp and catfish using the 'in' bait, which was a chunk of hard roe from recently cleaned bass or crappie. Some went bass and crappie fishing in the boats, and the powerful motors roared up the lake to spots twenty or more miles from the dock.

There we cast among the stumps and tree tops, changing lures and rates of retrieve continually in an attempt to find the 'formula' for the day. Sometimes we blanked out, sometimes we had a reasonable stringer to bring back with us. We knew, deep down, that every fish was going to be hard won. On the first day Charlie Minor, an extremely experienced guide, remarked, 'Hell, Fred, we just gotta get this smell of skunk out of the boat.' I looked at him a bit queerly at first and then I realized that he was drawing attention to the fact that were were 'skunked' – i.e. fishless!

We finally made it with a couple of 'taker' bass, but we worked on it hard before success came. To go back with an empty stringer, regardless of these exceptional conditions, would have been a blow to Charlie's pride and he could not have that. Nor could 'Wink' Winkleman and Todd Goodheart, our other two guides. They, too, cracked the whip daily and encouraged us to fish hard during our relatively brief periods of actual fishing.

A local angler sat on the docks one evening and caught three carp between five and nine pounds. He spiked them on a stringer and tied them to the jetty before killing them to take home for the table. Smoked carp, he told us, were delicious, and Kevin Clifford almost cried. Kevin loves carp and there were rumours afoot that he sneaked down to the dock one night to release some of the fish already strung during the day. We never proved it, but at least one eleven-pounder disappeared overnight. Kevin was suspect because at one stage he defied American protests and released a nine-pounder immediately after capture. 'No one,' he said, 'is going to spike *this* one on a stringer and, delicious or not, it is going back!'

The Americans tried hard to understand how we feel about one of our most popular fishes but, in a country where carp are regarded as vermin, the message was hard to convey. Nevertheless, having seen our ten-foot carp rods and marvelled at their casting and fish-handling qualities, one or two American anglers began to see the carp in a new light. They were certainly impressed with their fighting qualities and I believe that if a method could be devised whereby carp could be caught on lures, their carp fishing would take on an entirely new dimension. That would be good, for there is an abundance of sport almost entirely ignored all over the USA.

For two nights I slept on Judge Thresher's houseboat moored at Rocky Branch, and for one of those nights it snowed heavily and unceasingly. At 6 a.m., for a reason I shall never really know, I left the comfort of my warm bed and, with bare feet paddling in the thin carpet of snow, cast three lobworms into the deep water off the bows. I leaned the rod on the rails and in the warm cabin I drank coffee while I watched the rod through the glass doors. Suddenly it bent down towards the water, rattling on the rails, and with the light from the docks reflecting against the falling snow I played a ten-pounder to a standstill and brought it to net. I crawled back into the warm bed as the first light of dawn began to break, and I reflected that I'd played carp in bare feet before, but never in a blizzard!

Over breakfast that morning Jack Erhesman and Dan Gapen told me they wanted to take some pictures of carp and left the dock with instructions for me to go to work. They would be back at noon, they told me, and they returned on the dot, in time to photograph me with a freshly caught thirteen-pounder. I put on a 'big dog' act, but I have to confess that this fish, too, hooked itself while I was relaxing with a cup of coffee! The snow had gone by then and the sun was bright and strong. It seemed incredible that I could have caught two carp in such a short time in conditions that were so unbelievably different. But that's how it is in Arkansas.

Jim Bagget, the Chief Game Warden, remarked at the time that Beaver Lake was the 'damnedest fishin' hole in the United States'. Having fished there many times before and since I know what he meant.

From the actual number or weight of fish caught, the trip could hardly have been called a success, but in all other respects it was just about the greatest success story of all time. Thanks to some incredible organizing by Bill Hughes and the generosity of those wonderful people of Rogers, Arkansas, my party saw American hospitality at its very best. We were loaned a car for the two weeks by a local garage owner, our licence fees were paid for us, we were given guided tours of various centres of interest, we were flown all around the Ozark hills in a private plane, and we were entertained lavishly almost every night in true Arkansas style.

We still talk about it today whenever we meet, and I have been pressed several times to organize a similar trip again. Perhaps, one day, when I have more time. . . .

I had first fished at Table Rock in 1967. Part of the time I was in Oklahoma and part of the time in Missouri, but not until the year of the conducted tour did I learn that Table Rock Lake covers part of three states – the third one being Arkansas.

It is a famous lake and noted for its fine bass fishing. The largemouths grow big, but the fish that always impressed me were the white bass. These are shoal fish that lie deep during high summer and periodically come to the surface to feed on the shad that provide the bulk of their food. It is a sight to be remembered; the water explodes as the white bass go to work.

Boat motors that have been idling suddenly roar into action and cut out within easy casting distance of the edge of the shoal. Then it is action, action all the way. Every cast with a small spinner or jig takes a fish and there is no time for finesse. These fish may weigh up to four pounds or more, but they average perhaps half that, and they have to be 'horsed' away from the shoal and hustled into the boat. The real skill lies in casting to the fish on the very edge of the shoal. That way you can keep catching them, but if you throw into the middle of that boiling, churning mass of fish you put them down and lose them. In any event the action is usually short – but very sweet.

I returned there simply because I wanted to catch some white bass again but my friends Al Kennedy and Bob Cowan told me as soon as I arrived that I could not expect that kind of action in April. The fish were widespread and had to be hunted in ones and twos in the deeper water. Occasionally, I was told, you could find a pocket of fish and take a limit (thirty fish) in a very short time, but not often. I shared a boat with Al and Bob. Six other friends shared two more boats and we went forth full of hope.

We worked the stumps and the shore line of the old river bed with small bar-spoons and jigs all morning with very little return, and I confess that I found it hard going. I remembered the carp back at Rocky Branch and I wondered, perhaps, if I would have been better off fishing for those.

I had heard that these white bass really hit lures hard in spring, but I was disappointed in the few 'pecks' I had. Few fish were being caught anywhere, however, and I suffered in silence. By lunch time I had taken a couple of white bass, one of them close to two and a half pounds. After lunch we fished the deeper water in the middle channel and did a little better. By normal Table Rock standards our catch wasn't too great, but it was an interesting experience for me. I had ten fish myself, including two rainbows that had to go back, but of them all only five were 'keepers'.

At the end of the day the stringers, though not full, were at least loaded, and the fish were quickly and expertly filleted at the water's edge by our professional guides. Mine were deep frozen for me to take back to Illinois for my fish-starved friends. They were duly appreciated.

It never ceases to amaze me how delicious American freshwater fish are. No one there would want to fish, I'm sure, if there was any question of having to return the catch at the end of the day. American fishers do put fish back, of course, but generally speaking they are fish surplus to the limit. They are kept alive on the stringer and the best are retained for eating. I once thought the American stringer was a diabolical instrument, but now I know that, as far as big fish go, it is better than the best of our keep-nets. The fish usually lie quietly once they are tethered. None of their natural slime is rubbed off as it is in our keep-nets and they can be released later apparently none the worse for wear. I have used them a lot myself in recent years and I like them. Along with transistorized sonar units, downriggers, bucktail and streamer flies, electronic thermometers and modern plugs, they are items of equipment I have found invaluable for fishing in many parts of the world. If I had to name the item of tackle I have found most useful, however, I would nominate the American weedless jig-spinner. I learned how to use it in Arkansas, and its deadliness became immediately apparent.

Imagine if you can a forest of trees, almost completely submerged so that only the top branches are out of the water. This may give some idea of the unbelievable snags that lie beneath the surface of USA man-made impoundments. Some of the trees are so close together that there is hardly room to scrape the boat between them. That is where the bass lie and that is where the lure has to be tossed and retrieved. It is an almost impossible situation, demanding strong tackle and deadly accurate casting, but with good weedless lures it can be done. A number of English anglers have studied similar situations here and have devised, as I have, a few fairly snag-proof pike lures, but none is as effective as the latest American weedless jig-spoon. I brought large numbers of them back with me for fishing around some particularly frightening tree stumps where I knew the pike lay thick. They proved to be more than good enough for our pike. Though I tried very hard at one time to prove that they would get caught up just like any other lure, I just could not get myself snagged. They slid through branches just as smoothly as a hookless tackle, but their single, shielded hooks have tremendous quality and hooked fish seldom come adrift.

I learned a lot at Table Rock, and I have been able to apply much of it to my English fishing. I hope to go on learning and my attitudes meanwhile are slowly changing. I find myself preferring the American style of fishing (which is in truth an exercise in hunting) to the traditional English style of waiting for bites. Today I hunt my pike with lures rather than with baits and I regularly take fish for the table as I have always done and as is my right as a hunter.

7

Good Sport, Good Friends

I had belonged to a small club having access to some carp fishing and in years past it had been the club's policy to have an annual rabbit pie supper. This function obviously died out with the rabbits themselves at the beginning of the myxomatosis era, but it still came up at one of the club meetings. What a pity we could not have one of the old rabbit pie suppers, said an old member. Those really were the days!

The club's president, who owned the land and the pits where we fished, surprised us all by saying that he had plenty of rabbits. They only needed catching, he said, and we could have our rabbit pie supper if we knew how to get the rabbits. He would, he said, be glad to see the back of them.

I knew Malcolm Baldwin as a young club member at the time, and I knew him also to be interested in rabbits and ferreting. The result was that we both agreed to take out our respective ferrets and try to provide enough rabbits for a club supper the following week.

At the outset we were very much in tune with each other and our thoughts were almost identical. We both recognized an ability in the other and, because we appeared to have an immediate respect for the other's way of working, a friendship developed that remains, despite almost a quarter of a century age gap, to this day.

Working territory that was new to both of us was not easy and some of the rabbits were in deep, but we were of the same mind at once. Trust the ferrets to work hard and come back eventually, but do not be afraid to tackle a difficult situation. It took us all day and we had a long hold up with four young ferrets working frantically underground, but we ended up with twenty-six prime rabbits and eight very exhausted but utterly happy ferrets.

So began a friendship that revolved around field sports generally, but when autumn came my great pleasure stemmed from rabbiting with Malcolm. He and I worked well together setting wires, running long nets, working ferrets, shooting pheasants or catching trout. He is a better shot; I think he would agree that I am the more experienced angler, but between us we have an almost telepathic understanding that has kept us and our families well fed over the years.

Between the wars it had not been uncommon for sportsmen and farmers to move rabbits around and establish new communities where none existed before. Brush piles were surrounded by wire netting and wild rabbits were caught and released in the compound. In their attempts to burrow out of their confinement, the rabbits dug tunnels and started underground systems that eventually became new warrens. In later years it became illegal to move rabbits from one area to another, but I did not know that when I became involved in a transfer myself.

It all started when a farmer friend remarked that he hadn't a rabbit left on the farm. He waved a hand across the Vale from his house on the hill and said he'd got used to seeing them about and that he'd like to see a few more back again.

At about that time, in early May I believe it was, another farmer friend, John, from five miles away (less as the crow flies) began complaining bitterly that he'd got too many rabbits.

'I'm up to my ears in rabbits,' he said. 'For pity's sake come over and sort 'em out for me!'

'Yes,' we said. 'We'll come over September time and make an early start. Can't do anything about it at present, of course. There's no way we can use ferrets or wires at this time of year, you understand.'

John didn't understand.

'They're all along my drive,' he howled. 'They're tearing up the garden and eating me out of house and home. I can't *wait* till September!'

'OK,' we said, 'leave it with us and we'll try something else.'

Studying the terrain by daylight, it became apparent that John did indeed have a rabbit problem in one very localized area. There were two main buries, fairly close together in a small paddock, and the feeding area was obviously in the next field on the far side of the drive. It was, in fact, a perfect drop for a long net and a few nights later, when the moon was down and the wind was right, we went to work. The 100-yard string covered both buries and, while I stayed with it, Malcolm sneaked out of the back entrance to the far side of the feeding field and quartered back to me.

I'd been very careful about the drop because this was going to be something new even for me. I had a sack with me and the object was to put the rabbits into this sack alive and release them over on the other farm. In normal circumstances it's easy to handle rabbits once they've hit the net. They very quickly become dead rabbits and give no more trouble! All you do is grasp the rabbit (net and all) around the neck behind the ears with the left hand, put the heel of the right hand under its chin and push back. Snick; it's dead! That is a quick and humane way of killing rabbits in any situation, but here I was trying to extricate live ones; and unless you've ever tried to unravel a kicking, balled-up mass of fur and mesh that seems to be all arms and legs in utter darkness, you'll never really appreciate the difficulties involved.

By the time Malcolm got back to me I had three safely in the sack, which I was kneeling on to keep closed, and trying desperately to unravel the fourth, which had somehow managed to snarl up the string between every one of its toes and claws. Eventually I developed a fit of the giggles, which only made matters worse, and I sent Malcolm off to extricate the others which were fairly pounding the net to my left and right.

He duly came back with four others and, with my stubborn beast also in the sack by now, we tied it up, picked up the string, and made our way across to the other farm. It was then, and only then, that I began to wonder about the legality of it all. What if we were stopped and questioned? It was, after all, nearly 2 a.m.

In my present mood I imagined myself explaining to the officer of the law.

'Well, yes, actually we've been putting this rabbit net down and we've got eight live rabbits in the boot which we're going to carry half a mile across two meadows and put down some holes while it's still dark!'

And I imagined also the lawman saying 'Would you mind blowing into this bag, sir?' I developed another fit of the giggles!

Fortunately we were not stopped, nor were we questioned. We did our job without let or hindrance and eight rabbits (all pregnant does, on inspection) were duly released in an old, unused bury.

Within two days Bill began reporting signs of rabbits about once more and, as the summer progressed, he made mention of seeing a 'nice lot of young-uns'.

It was only after 'Harvest-Home' that the full significance of the situation hit him. There was a frantic 'phone call one evening and Bill howled down the line in a kind of anguish.

'Fred,' he bellowed. 'I'm up to my ears in rabbits. For pity's sake come on over and sort 'em out for me!'

Records show that we killed sixty-four rabbits around the immediate release area that winter. And we've had good hunting there ever since.

Samuel the farmer (that wasn't his real name) is no longer with us, and even when he was we didn't care much for him. He was mean and unpleasant. He had a farming operation that was highly efficient in many respects, and he had more than his share of worldly goods, for which he had, no doubt, worked very hard. No one begrudged him that except, perhaps, his cowman, who couldn't remember when he'd last had a day off, but who cared too much for his stock to do anything about it.

What irked us about Samuel was the way he'd get out of his Bentley on market days and complain bitterly between double brandies about how poor he was, how his profits were all shot to hell and how he was being eaten alive with rabbits. We knew the bit about the rabbits to be true. Samuel had thousands of them on the sprawling hills that made up much of his farm. The trouble was that, although he didn't want the rabbits, he wasn't prepared to let someone else have them. The thought of anyone having something for nothing off his farm burned deep in his soul and he clammed up every time anyone mentioned the subject of rabbiting!

Des, my old school friend, had managed to catch him in a better mood once and came away with the strange proposition of being given permission to kill the rabbits provided he paid half a crown for each one he killed. The going rate for rabbits at that time was half a crown! We could have bought all we needed at that price and, although we were motivated mainly by sport and not profit, it didn't seem to us like a very good deal. Those rabbits were down almost deep enough to have pouches and somehow we didn't fancy paying for work. We decided to let Samuel keep them.

It was late September when Des and I met Lionel the cowman in the local.

'The guvnor's going away for the weekend next week,' he said. 'Leaving Friday night; coming back Sunday night. Why don't you come over and trip up a few rabbits?'

Why not indeed? We knew the lie of the land because we had permission to kill rabbits on nearby farms and on the Saturday afternoon we went over with a gross of snares.

We weren't experts at the game but we knew the basics. The shiny brass wires had been dulled with vinegar because we were convinced that it made a difference. The pegs were short, stubby and well mudded so that the tops wouldn't show when they were driven flush into the ground. The prickers had been made, split and dried well in advance and were now stiff, sharp and manageable.

We looked over the vast warren, and marvelled at its size. The ground was foul; the only plants growing in the vicinity were nettles in abundance, and even those were paddled down flat in many places. The 'jumps', those recognizable spots where rabbits for some inexplicable reason hop with such precision that the long grass is flattened in front of and behind it, were in evidence everywhere. It was a temptation to litter the area with snares willy-nilly, but we'd been taught better than that. We knew that, although the jumps were fewer and less pronounced farther out, they would offer better chances of success.

Rabbits leave their holes cautiously and proceed slowly out to the feeding area. Anyone who has watched by day will know this to be true, and the same applies after dark. Snares are more likely to be sensed when rabbits are proceeding cautiously than when they're well on the move. Experience has shown that snares seldom tighten effectively when contacted near the bury or warren. They are also prone to being knocked aside and rendered ineffective because of the way the tracks or runs crisscross each other. And there's no doubt whatsoever that one rabbit caught close to the bury will send out warning signals and encourage others to stay at home.

A hundred yards or more from the warren, runs begin to split up into several 'main lines' and these in turn break up into less defined tracks leading off in all directions. By the time rabbits have reached this point, they are split up, proceeding along their own chosen routes confidently, and less likely to spread alarm. This is where the wires should be set, and where we, in fact, decided to go to work.

We worked roughly to a checkboard pattern as nearly as possible, putting down in straight lines over a wide square, twelve snares long by twelve snares wide. It isn't really as complicated as it sounds, and even in pitch darkness it's possible, by taking good landmarks, to walk up each line of snares without missing any. We set them, as we'd always done, just over a hand high and with a loop big enough to clear a clenched fist. Then we dropped our bags in the old straw barn where we'd planned to spend the night and went down to the local to pass the time.

There are, of course, many different approaches to this kind of rabbiting, but I think it's fair to say that the numbers caught are seldom proportional to the number of snares put down.

I have an old friend whom I would almost guarantee to catch three rabbits in three snares every time he set them. That is because he knows instinctively where best to set his limited supply. From then on he would be setting on less likely ground and his success average would drop as the number of snares increased. There are only so many 'perfect sets' in a given area. Once these are covered the success rate has to drop, which is why, despite our gross of wires, we were hoping for a success rate of little more than one in ten. We did not consider ourselves smart enough to expect much more, and we were more than pleasantly surprised to pick up nineteen rabbits when we walked round before midnight. (We walked round, should anyone wonder why we disturbed the night feed, for reasons of humanity and common sense. We wanted to dispatch the rabbits quickly, but we also wanted them whole and not half-eaten by foxes.) We legged and hung them round the barn to cool off, having reset the wires once more, and then took a short nap before going round again.

In all, that night, we took forty-nine rabbits, and then sat petrified in the barn as we watched Samuel's Bentley pull into the farm as dawn broke! He had returned long before time and we were obliged to remain concealed and hope that he would go to bed. Having driven home from Devon through the night (we knew where he'd been) it was on the cards that he would be tired, and we were relieved naturally to see the upstairs light go on. We gave him half an hour, checked the area, picked up the remaining wires, sneaked through the farmyard with our load and made our escape. Carrying twenty-five rabbits on a bicycle isn't easy, and going downhill it is positively dangerous, but we laughed the whole journey home.

Those snares, bought especially for that venture, cost three halfpence (old money) each. I still have over a hundred of them left and occasionally put them down to try and relieve a difficult situation. They would have paid for themselves a thousand times had I sold what they've caught over the years and they're still catching. But they've never produced as many rabbits or as much fun in one night as they did when we put one over on Samuel. I think of that occasion with pleasure every time I take them down from their peg.

'That old straw rick by the gate in the first field is riddled with rabbits,' said Jim the farmer. 'The straw's no good for anything much and it's got to go, but I'd like to get rid of the rabbits in it first if possible. Any ideas?'

Malcolm and I went to look over the situation. The straw bales were stacked high and there were signs of rabbits well up and low down near the ground. An impossible ferreting situation, we thought, but one that could be handled with a bit of thought, preparation and hard work.

It meant, of course, that every bale would have to be moved individually and that all avenues of escape would have to be blocked. No point in moving several hundred bales if the rabbits were going to sneak out while the last ones were being lifted. Which is what could easily happen in such a situation.

We couldn't get a long net completely round the rick. The hedgerows were too close to make it possible, but we were able to block the escape route effectively on three sides. We set the net well out – twenty yards or more from the rick. Then, starting at the very top, we lifted down the bales one at a time and began building a wall with them, completely surrounding the rick. We blocked all gaps with loose straw and, as the wall grew, the height of the rick decreased. Here and there we encountered forms and warm patches where rabbits had been lying, but saw no sign of the rabbits themselves. As we'd hoped, they were making their way downwards as we removed their cover from the top. None broke or made a run for it.

The wall was three bales high when the first rabbit made an escape bid and, finding all routes cut off, it tried to climb the wall. Sheer speed took it two bales high and then it went round the circular wall like a motor cyclist on the wall of death! I touched it twice myself. It wriggled free from Malcolm's embrace, dodged between Jim's legs, then, incredibly, located a tiny space we'd all overlooked between two bales, and squeezed through. It escaped up the hedgerow and I believe we all secretly congratulated it despite the work we'd done.

With the wall four bales high it became necessary to toss the remaining bales over the top of it. Left inside the ring they would form a step which would quickly be exploited and used as a 'launch pad' by any rabbits that remained. It is not easy tossing dry, rotting bales of straw over the top of a wall four bales high! It is even more difficult if the rotten string breaks when it is at its height. But it had to be done. The wall face had to be kept sheer to contain the escapees.

From now on each bale was lifted cautiously and the gap beneath inspected for signs of booty. The rick itself was two bales lower than the wall when the second rabbit broke. It too 'rode the wall of death' but, after much whooping, shouting and rugby-style tackling on our parts, it was finally caught and dispatched. A bale disintegrated as I lifted it clear above Malcolm's head. He disappeared momentarily under a cloud of chaff and emerged almost immediately with a grin and a struggling rabbit in his hand. Before he could dispatch it, two more broke from beneath his feet and chaos reigned for several minutes until they too were caught.

The air inside the wall grew thicker as the dusty bales were disturbed. Breathing was difficult, vision somewhat reduced, but every few minutes excitement overruled all as the ducking, weaving rabbits were chased round and round the arena. I've had more successful days' rabbiting but I don't remember any that were as noisy or as utterly insane as this one.

A strong buck broke from the centre when the rick was down to its last layer. I held it briefly but it kicked itself free, and the others all but had it several times. It too gathered speed and finally took to the wall where, unbelievably, its increased speed took it higher and higher until finally, avoiding all three pairs of grasping hands, it threw itself clear over the top.

In blind panic it took off across the meadow, hit the long net at full stretch and, by some strange twist of fortune, bounced out of it on the far side. The 'standing gun' we had positioned for such an emergency missed! The last we saw of that buck was its white scut as it disappeared over the brow of the hill to our spontaneous round of applause. If ever a creature deserved to escape, that one did. I wonder just what odds could be laid against it happening again?

Rabbits are remarkably capable of pulling off tricks like that, and their ability to win out when the odds are truly stacked against them is remarkable. I cannot help but believe that this ability means their future is assured.

There was once a time when I became angry if I lost a rabbit. Not because of the loss but rather because I felt I'd been careless in not anticipating the possibility. Today I'm as wise in rabbit behaviour as I'm ever likely to be, but still the odd one escapes me. I no longer become angry. I bow to a creature more adept than I in the business of survival!

When the last bale was lifted the total rabbit tally stood at thirteen captured and two escapees which, considering the fact that we'd used only our bare hands, was a fair achievement. The long net and the standing gun had not added to the score in any way. We'd have done just as well without them as it happens, but it's easy to be wise after the event.

For the next two days we had sore throats and croaky voices, which we naturally put down to the amount of dusty chaff we'd inhaled. The truth, however, was that we'd simply shouted ourselves hoarse!

An opportunity to take over a small, run-down shoot comprising about 270 acres of arable land with ample cover came my way at the end of harvest one year, and, although I could not afford to take it on myself, I accepted the offer at once. I gathered together a small group of friends, showed them the territory and convinced them that the prospects were excellent. Between us we found the rent and I paid my full corner like all the rest. I thought from the outset that matters of policy would be decided democratically; but it did not work like that.

'We'll leave it to you, old man,' said the others. 'Do what you think is best.'

The obvious rules of safety were naturally observed in their entirety but they were never mentioned for the simple reason that we all knew of their importance. Otherwise I never made any serious rules because I do not like rules. I believe that any small club or syndicate, whether it has to do with fishing, shooting, or whatever, runs better without them. Harmony and satisfaction are better achieved without a list of what is or is not allowed, and the only rule I would ever consider necessary would probably read 'Do not do anything that is likely to spoil things for someone else'. That covers it all, and where a group of sportsmen are all of the same mind it becomes a simple law unto itself. Anyone who does not agree does not belong!

Fortunately I had Malcolm Baldwin to help and the cooperation of the farmer's son who took care of most of the vermin in return for the chance to shoot with us. In the main, however, the chores were taken for granted and undoubtedly looked upon as personal labours of love by the others. They were probably right. There is more to shooting than a pile of birds at the end of the day, and Malcolm and I regarded the other aspects of the operation as being of much greater importance.

The decision regarding birds was always left to me. Numbers, age, time of year, and so forth, were extremely important considerations and, in my opinion, should have been decided democratically if only to get me off the hook when things did not work out the way they should have done. I tried it all ways, and time being my most important commodity, I finally opted for the purchase of ex-laying-pen adults to be released in June. I put it to the others when I first considered the idea.

'Shall we try it?' I asked, hoping for something positive in the way of an answer. And again they said, 'We'll leave it to you, old man. Do what you think is best.'

I reckoned it was a cop-out on their part (as indeed it was) but I went ahead and tried it, and it worked. It worked better than any other programme I had tried before, and it required so little of my time that I was greatly relieved. I missed an evening's trout fishing when the first batch was put down and Malcolm and I had to do a great deal of water hauling and grain shifting to try and hold the birds, but apart from that there was nothing much to it.

Fortunately we had one particularly thick covert which we had decided to leave as a sanctuary for most of the time and it was in this sanctuary that we released the adult birds. There was a risk of foxes getting at them before they could roost, since it is said that these adult birds cannot fly due to having been pinioned, but I never found this to be the case. In fact, releasing them (under the watchful eye of the game farmer himself in the first instance) was done in such a manner as to keep the birds on the ground. Even so, several hen birds took off, circled the wood and happily flew back in again.

There were eggs in the baskets when I took delivery and I became convinced that some of those adult birds brought off small late broods despite all the odds stacked against them.

Pheasants are reputed to be stupid birds, but somehow ours managed to survive the incredible number of foxes around. I dare not think of the numbers we shot over the years (rightly or wrongly, but I think rightly) because if I did, I might be scared to buy another bird for the rest of my life. Many would say I should have ringed the birds I released in order to keep tally on the returns, but I never did so, because I was really only concerned with keeping numbers up, and I looked upon my annual stocking programme as a topping-up operation.

We were indeed very fortunate in that for five years the guns never failed to kill more birds than were put down! A tall statement, but an absolutely honest one, and one which called for an increased number of stock birds each year because mine was a simple philosophy. I treated our shoot in much the same way as the trout fisheries' manager treats his waters. I did not put down birds to shoot, but to replace those we had shot.

We may not have held the actual birds we put down (without ringing we could never know) but it did not matter. Someone else may have benefited from our conservation, but we in turn benefited from theirs, and over the years the number of birds per gun steadily increased. Which is part of what conservation is all about.

If every shooting man released the same number of birds he killed each year, irrespective of where or when, I think we might see a wider and better distribution all round. Not everyone would agree with me in that respect, and there are no doubt situations where it would be a waste of time and money to release birds anyway. I can imagine many shooting men asking why they should release birds for someone else to kill. A fair enough question I suppose, but my suggestion is only one of replacement. If a sportsman kills a brace of birds in a season, and then puts down a brace to compensate, it doesn't matter much where they go from there. And after all he did manage to get his brace somewhere!

Economically you could tear this idea to pieces, of course, but I believe it stands up well enough in other respects.

I put down the birds every year from June onwards – and we took it from there. I doubt if anyone knew how many birds I put down. No one ever asked and half the time I hardly remembered myself. My aim was never to kill large numbers, but rather to provide some good shooting throughout the season.

Most of the birds were walked up, but because we were fortunate in having two small coverts fairly close together and centralized, we were able to organize the occasional drive. Drive? It usually involved one gun and as many dogs as he could reasonably control, taking the long wood through to the standing guns at the far end. With more guns we could have killed more birds because our small numbers were unable to cope with those that broke to either side.

We knew this would happen and we knew that opportunities would be missed, but no one cared.

A successful 'drive' put a percentage of high birds over the guns, and, because it was almost one hundred per cent guaranteed that those birds would make for the bigger covert over their heads, unwritten rule no. 1 came into existence. Let us call the two coverts A and B. A was regarded, for the greater part of the season, as a sanctuary. We did not work it, but left the birds there in peace. So, birds driven over our guns from B were never taken behind. If they could not be taken forward they were left alone. It is but a short flight from B to A, and a bird taken behind inevitably fell into the sanctuary. This, of course, meant that the dogs had to go in and retrieve. Hunting a lost bird can be a lengthy business, particularly if it has not been killed cleanly, and an enthusiastic springer, with the whiff of a runner up his nostrils, would play havoc with resident birds. No one ever made rule no. 1, it just happened, but it is noticeable that someone or other always informed guests of its existence.

I cannot recall a day when we managed to walk the whole shoot. There were so many thick hedgerows to cover that it would have needed an early start and a late finish to do so. No one wanted to anyway, but because it was hard to decide upon the areas to be worked, rule no. 2 came into existence. A 'shoot bosun' was appointed at the beginning of every day's shooting to take full charge, rightly or wrongly, of the complete strategy. He directed operations, he placed guns, he dictated and he was obeyed to the letter. All of which made for a great deal more pleasure than a set procedure which can become boring. And it was fun.

The best laid schemes, the craftiest of ploys, often failed and the wrath of the guns descended upon the bosun at the end of the day. It was important to have someone to blame for the day's misfortunes over the evening tot and the appointment of the bosun did just that. Everyone else could have made a much better job of the day's organization, of course, but it was interesting to note that, next time round, no one ever actually volunteered for the job. The shoot bosun had his day of greatness thrust upon him by popular vote, and from then on he was on his own. No one disputed his orders, but whether or not he went home in a blaze of glory was truly in the lap of the gods. And if that poor unfortunate perchanced to pull off some brilliant shots himself to end the day as 'top gun', he was naturally accused of organizing the shoot with that end in view!

That was the fun side of it, and none of the complaints was ever taken seriously. The advantages of such an arrangement, however, were enormous. No two shooters think alike and we all learned a great deal more about the shoot in general because we followed so many odd procedures.

It was always our practice, for example, to work the outer hedgerows first with the idea in mind that any birds flushed would fly inwards to the covert, which we could then work at the end of the day. It was a policy we tended to accept without question until a newly appointed bosun decided that he wanted the covert beaten in the wrong direction at the very beginning of the day.

Far be it from any of us to question the decision. Except that without exception we all howled him down!

'They'll break in all directions,' we pointed out, 'and we don't have enough guns to handle such an operation.'

'That's right,' he said. 'They'll break all over the place and we'll work the hedgerows where they've settled. *Then*, they'll be spread out more and we can take them one at a time. Any that are missed will more than likely make back for the covert anyway.'

It so happened that he was absolutely right and we ended that late-season shoot with an above-average bag. I doubt very much if we would ever have considered such an approach but for rule no. 2.

Rule no. 3 arrived because of my own feelings about game birds generally and, although I did not try to enforce it, I made the point that pheasants with their necks pulled are no longer strictly 'game'.

Even on the best of organized shoots there are bound to be runners that need dispatching quickly and humanely when retrieved, but in my opinion nothing looks worse than a pheasant with its neck stretched. A game stringer is the ideal carrier on a rough shoot (far better, in my view, than a traditional bag), but a bird with a broken neck can hardly be carried on one. The skin stretches and, with no bone structure to take its weight, the bird deteriorates, if only in looks. At worst the head parts company eventually and the result can only be described as a bloody mess. I have seen birds held by the feet and killed like chickens. I have seen them held by the head and swung round like a rodeo cowboy's lasso. Both methods kill quickly and positively but sometimes lack of experience, haste, or over-enthusiasm pulls the head off completely. Try hanging one of these on a stringer!

There is a very simple answer to the problem and, while it needed the odd demonstration from time to time on my part, I finally convinced the other shooters that the best way is to bite the bird's head. It isn't anything like as gory as it sounds. The skull is simply cracked like a nut, the bird is killed instantly and remains game in the true sense of the word. For a time, on odd occasions, someone a little squeamish passed a bird over to me for dispatch and I never made an issue of the procedure, but very noticeably, the number of stretched necks became fewer and fewer each season.

Whether or not birds with broken necks were strictly game or not did not bother me. Today, as always, my own birds are invariably dressed out on the same day as they are shot. That is the way I prefer it. If and when I give away a brace of birds, however, I want them to look like pheasants – not vultures.

Ours was a small and very happy shoot. Our membership remained the same because we were all of the same kind. Safety, harmony, good fellowship, sensible organization and consideration all round were more important than a pile of birds at the end of the day, but those attributes went a long way towards achieving that also.

For seven years I ran the shoot successfully and in the main it provided good sport for all concerned. It is one of the harder facts of life, however, that farming has to become more and more intensive if it is to be profitable and intensive farming is not conducive to good shooting. Our hedgerows grew thinner and fewer and, as farming methods improved, our bird cover grew less. It became obvious that the number of walked-up birds was going to diminish rapidly and that we were likely to be left with wood shooting only. We gave it up reluctantly and attempted to develop a fresh shoot on 600 acres farmed by a close friend. He too was a very efficient farmer, however, and we gave up trying to hold birds after two attempts. Malcolm and I retained the shooting rights and have them still to this day.

We killed very few pheasants over the years, but those 600 acres have produced many rabbits, large numbers of pigeon and not a few hares and wild duck of several kinds. More than that, however, it has given us freedom to roam at will and without restriction. That in itself is worth more than a full game bag.

I was introduced to the River Test by a fine old sporting gentleman – one Bill Nash of Great Missenden – and, as a result, Bernard Aldrich, the river keeper on Broadlands Estate, became a close personal friend. He was an understanding man who told me much about the fishery in general, and I later took a rod on the trout fishery which he had developed in a small carrier stream on the river. It was a stream demanding of stealth, low cunning and the approach of an Indian warrior rather than the skill of an expert caster. I failed to catch a single fish only once. I took many limits when the going was easy, and I struggled for a brace many times during the dog days of summer, but I loved (and still love) the carrier, its delightful situation and all that goes with it. Artificial no doubt, since the water was stocked with rainbow trout and brown trout quite regularly, but much of today's trout fishing is dependent upon introduced fish, and put-and-take fisheries have become the norm rather than the exception.

I could tell of fantastic days there. I could make a big deal out of the day when I caught a nine-pounder before the very eyes of the critics who told me I never stood a chance. I could tell of the day when I took eight fish by 7.30 a.m., and I could report with great drama the day when in two consecutive casts I took a brown trout weighing six pounds thirteen ounces and a rainbow trout weighing one ounce less. From my own point of view they were days to be remembered, and there were many others too. Bearing in mind once again, however, that catching fish is not the be all and end all of my fishing, I choose to recall one of the lesser days in this book. I choose to tell it because the day in question turned out to be one of changing fortunes. We all experience them, and I am sure that many other anglers are as aware of them as I have always been. Days, for example, that start off badly and days when the early hours are hopeless, but which end up in success, deserved or otherwise, later.

I had had my eye on a big trout under a small bridge for a long time. It had remained screwed down to the bottom in a situation that defied the use of regular fly-casting tackle. It was, to all intents

and purposes, an impossible fish, and I studied it from a prone position week after week without finding a way of getting a fly to it. It
was not a scary fish; it was so safe it didn't know how to be scared.

I went to look at it one day in July and the familiar shape was
missing from the bottom. Someone, I thought, had somehow or
other managed to extract it, and I wondered how. I leaned over,
hand on a thin branch of a nearby tree, to peer deeper; and – half-
expectedly – the branch broke. Falling face first into the water is not
funny at 6.30 a.m.

The trout, if it had been there at all, was obviously somewhere
else by the time I had scrambled out of the water, so I moved on and
caught a couple more. I simply had to go back to the bridge again
later, however – just to satisfy myself that my trout really had gone.
I took up the prone position again and heard a distinct plop. Ripples
spread outwards and I realized that my trout was actually rising
about a couple of feet from my ear. But there was still no way I could
get at it by conventional methods. I could not cast to it without
scaring it and so I took a chance in another direction.

I should say at this point that I had put on a new leader earlier and that, to save time, I had not bothered with a needle knot, but had simply tied it on in the old-fashioned way. The significance of this fact will soon become apparent!

Removing the top joint of my rod and propping the bottom half against the bridge, I tried to let the fly drift naturally down to the fish for all of two feet, but even the top joint was too long for the job. So I took hold of the leader, told my brother Ken to stand by to take the rod if I should succeed in hooking the fish, and lowered the fly into the water. I had forgotten the rod was in two sections and Ken was desperately trying to put them together when the trout took. My reaction, either by luck, instinct, or blinding skill, was to jerk the leader just enough to set the hook. There was an almighty splash and I yelled out, 'Gotcha. OK mate, he's all yours.' And Ken almost wept.

'I ain't got the perishing rod together yet,' he wailed.

Have you ever tried playing a trout on a hand line? I did. And I must have done things right because, amazingly, the hook stayed in and the leader remained intact.

Ken got the rod together. The fact that the line was wrapped round it once went unnoticed, as he cranked away to take up the slack. The fish turned to go downstream as I struggled to stand up and grab the landing net, and there were thunderous splashings under the bridge.

'Let it go through,' I yelled, 'and I'll try to net it on the downstream end if I can see it.'

'How can I let the flaming thing go,' he bellowed, 'when the blasted leader knot's jammed in the tip ring? Would you consider tying proper leader knots in future please, dear brother?' Words to that effect at least.

The rod bent round and continued to bend until more than half of it was pointing in an alarming curve with the tip ring out of sight halfway under the bridge. Still the fish continued to thresh the surface, and still the tackle held.

'I'll just have to try and haul it back, that's all,' said Ken.

'Well, all right,' I yelled, 'but just haul it steady.' Silly things you say when panic rules! (Panic? This was about to be declared an official disaster area – at any moment.)

The landing net caught on the barbed wire and refused to budge. Brute force had no effect upon the incredible three turns it had somehow managed to execute in the excitement, and I was obliged to unravel it in a composed manner. Which takes some doing when there is a fish performing acrobatics, and a brother screaming for you to take your finger out!

How long it went on I do not really know. It is all a bit vague now, but I do remember making an almighty swipe at one of the splashes and ending up with the fish in the net. Then the hook dropped out!

We unravelled the rest of the line which was tangled (no, 'knitted' is the right word) around both my waders and Ken's fishing waistcoat.

I thought it was a five-pounder, but in fact it weighed less than four. I did not really mind about the weight; I was pleased I had finally managed to catch it. I would say that only sheer luck, plus some kind of disorganized teamwork, was responsible, for I would be the last person to take any credit or make any claims.

But I did forget all about my earlier ducking and felt that, perhaps, fortune was beginning to favour me again. There is truly more to fishing. . . .

8

The American Outdoors

Despite my simple life-style and my good fortune in having access to good shooting, rabbiting, fishing and other outdoor activities in the UK, my USA experiences made me anxious to return again, and again, and yet again. My American friend Ted Trueblood had a severe coronary in 1967; I had a mild one in 1969 and, although I recovered completely, I never forgot Ted's advice.

Do everything the doctors tell you to do, he advised, and you'll not only get over it, you'll find yourself doing even more than you managed before. It is all water under the bridge now, but the ghastly thoughts I experienced when lying in hospital, listening to the bleep of the electronic contraption to which I was attached, are still with me. Would I ever fish, shoot, ferret, or travel again? Would I ever see my dear friends in the USA again? Would I be a vegetable?

I need not have worried. I write this almost twelve years later and much has transpired since then, as will I hope become apparent. To say that I had a million friends, and that my wife need not have had a single financial worry had she accepted the flood of offers of help that came her way, would be no more than the truth. Everyone, including my employer and the editors for whom I worked, stood by me in my time of need. Friends and casual acquaintances offered practical help and, after a suitable spell of convalescence, I went back to the USA to renew old friendships.

I had met Bill Hughes before, and since we were both representatives in the fishing tackle industry ('tackle pedlars' in Bill's vocabulary) we had kept in touch. We had many enjoyable times together and they provided an opportunity for me to study the ways of the American promoter. Bill and I travelled thousands of miles together, fishing when opportunity arose, and talking of business methods when we could not relax in his beloved Arkansas. We had so very much in common, and if it is possible for two men to become lifelong friends overnight I'm sure Bill and I did just that. There could not have been a stronger bond of true friendship anywhere and we corresponded by tape between my annual visits. He would truly be worth a whole book in his own right. I can only mention our exploits briefly, but, since he is also a friend and admirer of Ted Trueblood, my ambition is for us all to get together again one more time before it is too late. We are so different and yet so much alike in many ways that I truly believe we have to make the effort. For my part, I love America and Canada and my experiences there have also made me realize that field sports, despite the attitudes of those who are 'anti' simply for the sake of being so, are as much a way of life out there as they are here. Men have been hunters since time began and all the tub-thumping in the world cannot make a man with hunting instincts change his mind. The expression, 'Don't knock it till you've tried it' is as American as corn bread, but applies the world over. And it happens to be a fact that field sports and field sportsmen have protected and saved more endangered species than all the political know-nothings put together, because they are con-servationists in the true sense of the word.

Bill Hughes was (and still is) a conservationist. He preached a gos-pel of conservation that was just as fervent as that preached by Ted Trueblood but in a different kind of way. He referred to himself as an 'Arkansas hillbilly with one leg shorter than the other through running round the Ozark Hills', but in fact he was a shrewd businessman whose country upbringing had taught him the need for conservation. Without that there could be no fish, without fish there would be no need for fishing tackle, and he was a tackle ped-lar! His motives were no different from mine. We both loved to shoot and fish, we both sold fishing tackle, and we both loved wild places when we could find time to visit them.

Lake Michigan at the time was rapidly becoming one of the world's largest freshwater fisheries. American and Canadian con-servation measures that included the transplanting of coho salmon parr had brought about the biggest transformation in the history of sport fishing. Lake Michigan had, over a period of less than five years, been elevated from a disgusting health hazard to an angler's paradise. The state of Michigan became a tourist attraction and began to prosper once more. Charter boat skippers plied for hire and sophisticated downrigger units were devised to take baits and lures down seventy, eighty, and ninety feet, to where the salmon were known to be. Sonar and depth thermometers were being used to locate shoals of fish and salmon fishing was being reduced to a true science. Bill regarded Michigan as his second home and, since he had studied the coho project from start to finish, it was small wonder that he waxed enthusiastic. He was in what he described as 'hog heaven' when he was sitting back in a charter boat cabin drinking cold beer and watching the downrigger tackles for the action to begin. He was determined that I should try it too, and we travelled together up to Saugatuck to meet up with two business friends, Charlie Redman and Marion Monroe, late one Friday evening.

We had arranged for charter boat skipper Marvin De Whitt to take us out next day and, over drinks in the worst motel I have ever had the misfortune to check into, we talked over the points I did not fully understand. I quickly saw the advantage of the downrigger and its separate line attachment. A light rod and reel carry the lure which is taken down to the required depth by a lead of up to fifteen pounds attached to a marked line. The fishing line is held in a quick-release clip which breaks away when a fish hits. The rod straightens and the fish is then played up on a limber rod and a line completely free of leads or ironmongery.

We chugged our way across the lake next morning with baits set at between fifty and a hundred feet. It was not rough, nor was it truly calm. I found myself hanging on for most of the time, but I knew at once that Charlie and Marion were having a whale of a time. Every so often a rod would pop and straighten and each time one or other would grab it, whoop with delight and crank a protesting coho to the surface. It was all good fun, but to be truthful there was precious little skill involved apart from that displayed by Marvin who did all but boat the fish himself.

Two days later we were again on Lake Michigan doing the same thing with Phil Spring from Muskegon. It was tough going and rough water made it unpleasant. I was not ill, though I expected to be seasick at any moment, but I was pleased to come ashore at last. I was even more pleased to join Phil and Bill next day in a scheduled bay on Lake Muskegon.

There we fished for bluegills until the sun went down and later, at Phil's house, with a million mosquitoes buzzing around our heads, we cleaned and dressed out a hundred under the garden hose. It was around midnight before they were all cooked in the two great skillets provided by Phil's wife. Then, with the mosquitoes gone and the moon high, we sat and gorged and gorged. . . . Bluegills and cold beer. There never was a better combination of food and drink!

I stayed at a small log cabin resort next day while Bill went coho fishing yet again. I had had my fill and I longed for a more intimate kind of fishing. Tom Opre, outdoor editor of the *Detroit Free Press*, was staying at the same resort and we struck up a friendship there that has lasted until this day. He too cared little for the heaving waters of Michigan and we whiled the day away together fishing for bluegills and swimming in a small private lake.

'Deep trolling is fun', he said at one stage, 'but it will never take the place of fishing!'

I knew what he meant, and although I have since learned much more of the Wolverine state, I never wanted to fish for lake coho again.

It had been a stormy day, and as I half dozed in my chair at Jacksonville, Illinois, I could still hear the rumble of thunder in the distance. St. Louis, some seventy miles away, had been hit three times by minor tornadoes during the day, and I was glad I was not out fishing.

Bill Hughes walked in. 'Get your butt out of that chair, neighbour,' he said, 'and get some tackle in the car. 'We're going fishing.'

'Fishing?' I said. 'On a night like this?'

'No, not tonight, tomorrow morning,' said Bill, 'but we'll have to travel down tonight.'

On the way down Bill told me we were going to fish Carlyle Lake, a flooded forest impoundment in Illinois, at the resort of Bob Coates who would act as guide and boatman. He would tell me no more about the fishing, however. 'Just wait and see,' was all he would say.

I unloaded the car after breakfast and put out the rods I thought we might need. All around me other fishermen were loading boats with all the trimmings that usually go with American fishing. There were cooler-boxes of iced beer, bait cans and tackle boxes, but I could see no real fishing rods or reels anywhere. All I could see were little two-piece cane poles, with tight lines of twine or thick nylon tied to their tips. Some of them had crude corks on, others were just hooked and shotted.

'You can leave all those fancy poles behind,' said Bob Coates, pointing to the fishing rods. 'You don't need 'em today. All we'll need are a few l'il ole cane poles.'

I thought he was joking, but he wasn't.

'Today,' said Bill, 'you're going to catch crappie in a different way.' He produced two buckets of live, shiner minnows and as he loaded them on board, he told me we were going 'minner dunkin' '.

I have caught crappie in the United States by many different methods. Three at a time on a fly rod, and singly on little jigs and spinners; I have caught them on worms, both real and plastic; I have float fished, spun and trolled for them; but I have never 'dunked minners' before. It was undoubtedly different, but it could hardly be called sport.

It did not set me hopping about with excitement, and even the shouts of 'I got me another son-of-a-bitch' from the other end of the boat failed to stir my imagination. It was meat-fishing pure and simple, and as far removed from American sport fishing as it could possibly be. I spent most of my time taking pictures, watching, and taking naps in the bottom of the boat. My excuse was that I was tired from recent travel and needed the rest.

All this does not suggest, however, that I do not recognize the special skills that go with that kind of fishing. It did not take me too long to discover that it was not quite as easy as it looked. How, for instance, do you lower a wriggling, live minnow through a tiny crack in an incredible underwater jungle of twigs, branches, limbs and trunks without getting snagged? Those submerged forests are so dense that it is quite impossible to manoeuvre a boat through them in many places. They are bad enough above the water line, but worse below it. At least you can see problems above the surface!

How do you differentiate between the pull of a crappie and the pull of a springy, underwater twig? How do you discipline yourself not to strike and set the hook when you feel a pull on the line? The

chances are that you will set the hook in one gigantic and immov-
able snag if you do. How, once you have learned to hook those
crappie gently, do you manage to steer them up through that tangled mass and coax them out of the water in one smooth movement
like pulling a cork from a bottle? And how, with strong winds caus-
ing the boat to toss like a cork on the ocean, do you manage to
handle a paddle, hang on to a branch and fish at the same time?

Bob and Bill were experts, and I was almost tempted to compete
but knew I was not up to it. I was puzzled, too, because in the past
Bill had had an aversion to bait fishing. He talked of bait fishers (as
opposed to lure fishers) in a way that sometimes made me feel like
something from under the nearest rock. Now, however, I know
differently.

I do not know how many minnows he and Bob used up that day.
They caught somewhere in the region of a hundred crappie and,
although at times they may have caught several fish with one bait,
they also lost a lot in the branches.

Minnows are reasonably priced in the United States where
fishing is big business. Shiner minnows are bred in huge ponds and
nurtured to usable size by intensive fish-farming techniques. It is a
year-round business, and millions of minnows are transported
thousands of miles all over the United States to waters like Carlyle
Lake. They are stored in rows of big, aerated tanks and are always
available at resorts and bait stores. They are hardy, but special insulated buckets are needed to keep the water on the boat cool so that
they stay lively even in very hot weather. I seldom use live bait, but
I could see that those buckets would be very useful in Britain.

In the late afternoon I was given a lift back to shore in another
boat and sat around drinking coffee and talking to other anglers
until Bob and Bill finally pulled ashore, triumphantly hauling their
huge stringer of fish. Iceboxes were filled at once and the task of
cleaning and gutting the fish began. That is not the nicest of jobs at
the best of times but when practised on the end of a floating dock,
rolling and bobbing up and down on a wave-swept surface, it is
horrific. Four anglers, standing ankle deep in water and wielding
razor-sharp knives, with slippery fish flopping around on the small
table and fish scales covering a very unstable platform, is not only
tricky but positively dangerous. I was glad when it was all over and

the fish stowed away, but I have to admit that the fish-fry we had later was out of this world. Ten of us sat and ate crisp golden-brown crappies until we were fairly bloated. American fish-fries are really something and are, of course, part of the American way of life.

At one time I was able to say quite truthfully that I had never been outfished in the United States. I held my own most of the time with some of the best anglers over there, and I remained secretly rather proud of the fact. Now I can no longer say it. When it came to minner dunkin' I was not only outfished but outclassed. I still say I was tricked into it but I would not have missed it for a thousand dollars. Nor would I give a nickel to do it again!

Charlie Bowen, Bill Hughes and I sat sipping iced sour-mash bourbon in Jacksonville, Illinois. It was a hot and humid evening and the small air conditioner was fighting a losing battle against the ideal corn-growing conditions.

'The squirrel hunting season opens tomorrow,' said Bill. 'Anyone fancy going?'

I had been educated previously into accepting that squirrels in the United States are strictly game. I had eaten them along with rabbit and could not remember an occasion when they had not tasted delicious. I expressed a desire to go, Charlie said that he would like to go also, and we decided to set off before dawn next morning.

It was still dark when we reached the wood and, while we waited for the light, Bill said it was a big area, perhaps, by English standards but not big enough for me to get lost. I was told to walk quietly, 'set a spell' occasionally, and wait for a squirrel to appear. After *two hours exactly*, I was to turn about and return to the start point where we would all meet.

I sat quietly on a big log and after a while heard a rustling in the tree above me. I caught a glimpse of the squirrel, lifted my borrowed twenty-bore auto to shoot and was somewhat disconcerted by the whine and thud of a bullet above my head. The squirrel dropped, and an American as big as a tank, completedly covered in camouflaged gear, came out of the bushes and claimed it. I moved on, quickly!

With the two hours up, I about-turned and made my way back to the starting point. I did it very easily, except that I was in the wrong place. I went back into the wood again to retrace my steps, but the more I moved around the more hopelessly lost I became.

The sun was up, the wood began to steam, and I began to feel ill as well as lost. I faced a ribbing if I called for help, and as there were other hunters in the wood I felt it would be unfair anyway. Then, in the distance, I heard the sound of buckets rattling and I headed towards them, hoping to get some directions from whoever was handling them. I negotiated a deep ravine, which was much too wide to jump, by clambering down one side and up the other; and as I staggered towards the clanking buckets, about 200 Illinois hogs, which had been operating self-feed hoppers, spotted me.

They stopped feeding when I inquired if anyone was present, put their heads down and charged. It may have been sheer friendship that made them do it, but I was now scared as well as sick and lost! I ran in panic, and I cleared the deep ravine I could not jump previously with feet to spare.

In the steaming heat of the wood I actually lost several pounds in weight, and, when I began to feel the first real twinge of panic, I put the gun to my shoulder and pulled three times. From miles away (we had been separated by six miles I learned later) I heard three faint reports come back and, after much negotiating of bogs and briars, I found my two friends again. It took two more hours, by which time I was totally exhausted.

I began to apologize to my friends for putting them to all this trouble, but Charlie interrupted and said that he too had been lost. And Bill, our host and guide, looked down at his feet, kicked a rotting stump and said, 'Aw hell, so was I!'

I squeezed the perspiration out of my shirt, took a long swig of coffee from Bill's flask and literally collapsed in the soft leaf mould of the wood. Had I not ventured into the wood before daylight I might not have been lost. Having the direction of the rising sun to guide me would have given me my bearings but, if I am completely honest, I have to admit that I was careless. I still tend to be that way even today, but when I know that I am going into thick woods or wilderness country, I am careful to take bearings and land-marks before I go.

That was an unsuccessful hunt; others since have been better, and nowadays in this country I never waste a squirrel. Indeed, I find it astonishing that countrymen who eat and enjoy rabbit go white at the thought of eating squirrel, because if you consider the diet of both animals and you take into account the corn, nuts and other good food devoured by squirrels, they are surely more likely to produce tasty meat than rabbits. Some game shots do shoot squirrels, of course. Some keep their tails for fly tying, others toss them into the undergrowth to rot. There are just a few who, like me, enjoy braised squirrel, fried squirrel, Brunswick stew or pâté, but we are in the minority and it hurts me to think of good food being wasted. I am quite sure that if more were prepared for the table and sampled, there would be more hunted and fewer wasted.

There is a difference. We are all agreed on the damage squirrels cause to trees, game and song birds. We are all agreed that they should be kept under control, but we shoot only if the opportunity comes during a day after other quarry. We should perhaps copy our American friends in this particular field. They have provided their grey squirrel with a season and a bag limit and I have yet to hear of any gluts or population problems. Perhaps if we recognized its edible qualities, gave it a season, and put it on the 'game' list, we would have no more problems ourselves.

My later travels with Ted Trueblood took me to many wild and

lonely places but none was more desolate or beautiful than the vast
area of sagebush, greasewood, rocks and sand that leads to the foot
of the Owyhee Mountains in the Oregon desert. I look upon this
desert as one of the few places left so far unaffected by herbicides,
pesticides, high-rise flats and commercial resorts. It has no value to
the land developer, there are no known resources to exploit and it
offers precious little in the way of comfort to the traveller, but it has
a rugged beauty of its own that appeals especially to the naturalist
and outdoorsman.

Taking a fishing rod into a desert may seem a little odd, but the
wherewithal to catch fish could, in the event of an emergency, be of
great importance. A trip of this nature is more of an exercise in
survival than a sport-fishing excursion; which is one reason why it
should not be undertaken lightly. An arid desert is no place to
become stranded without food, water or reliable transport, though
with proper care and planning there is no real danger.

The only safe way across is by four-wheel-drive truck. The track,
if you can find it, winds, climbs and occasionally disappears com-

pletely where rains have caused washouts. Then a compass becomes more useful than a defined track. By night the cold desert wind blows and by day the sun beats down out of an entirely cloudless sky. There is no respite except, perhaps, when fishing the great fifty-mile-long lake, whose headwaters are the old Owyhee river, to roll into the water and enjoy a dip. These are the memories of my first visit to the Owyhees.

Owyhee Lake was our destination and, once there, we knew we could survive almost indefinitely in the event of an emergency. There were fish to be caught and there was no shortage of water. It may well have been uninteresting, but a dull diet is better than starvation. Such a course was highly unlikely but torrential rains *can* come, and when they do there is absolutely no way out until the ground bakes hard once more. It is, therefore, important to be prepared, though with America's greatest outdoorsman as my host and teacher, I had no worries.

We had at least a week's emergency rations on board, and a great churn of water (it is about ten miles between water holes, and had it been necessary to proceed on foot at any time we had no wish to become dehydrated). We had modest medical stores, a snake bite kit (yes, there are rattlesnakes), an axe, shovel, tent, sleeping bags, cooking utensils and one bottle of bourbon (for emergencies only). We pulled a boat, an outboard motor, two spare tanks of petrol, fishing rods, reels, lures, flies and nets. We travelled light on frivolous items, heavy on essentials, but we did allow ourselves the luxury of an insulated box containing three dozen cans of pre-frozen

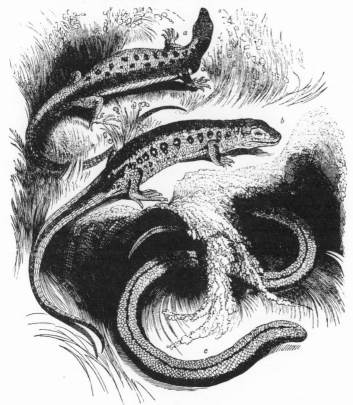

beer! American beer is disgusting stuff unless it is iced; ours was solid in the cans but quickly became drinkable when removed from the insulated box. This box, incidentally, served to store perishable food such as bacon, beef, butter and fresh vegetables until we ran out of them and had to fend for ourselves.

Much of the journey to the far end of the lake took us over terrain which kept the truck in low-low gear. We made, at best, ten miles an hour and occasionally had to take long detours over rocks and through sagebrush to skirt particularly bad washouts. At times it seemed to me, looking out of the passenger door down to the great gorge below, that we were in danger of sliding off; but the big tyres held and I eventually became more interested in the antelope, quail, chukar, meadowlarks (meadowlarks in a desert?), ground squirrels, lizards and other wildlife with which that vast and desolate area

abounds. I was nevertheless glad to make the final camp by the lake to ease my battered and aching bones in the warm water lake and wash away the accumulated trail dust.

Then it was time to gather driftwood and sagebrush along the lake shore and build a fire to cook the last of the fresh meat. Eating beef ribs cooked over sagebrush coals as the evening air cools and the smoke from the fire mingles with the smell of coffee, and the fish out on the lake begin to flip on the surface, is an experience never to be forgotten. You hold a wedge of bread in one hand, a great, succulent, crisp rib bone in the other; and you feel sorry for those poor creatures who sit at hotel tables toying with their Chateaubriand.

Hundreds of swallows, rock dwellers who build their mud colonies on the sheer cliff faces, skim the water for midges and gnats as evening approaches, and when the sun drops, prematurely, behind those great cliffs, the carp in the lake begin to roll on the surface and the catfish down below begin to bite. So you prop your baited rod up against a rock and, in the flickering firelight, wait for it to bend towards the water and indicate that tomorrow's breakfast is on the way. Catfish may not look very appetizing, but they are delicious. Then, as the night air cools you crawl into the sleeping bag, count the stars, and listen to the coyotes talking to each other across the great desert plain. During the night you waken and pull over an extra blanket because you are cold, and if that doesn't help, you move closer to the fire and replenish it.

At dawn you huddle round that fire until the coffee brews and the sun rises and both add their warmth to your shivering frame. Then you cook the bacon and the fish fillets in the big pan, eat them with freshly made hot pancakes, and start to live again. More coffee, and it's time to push out the boat and fish fairly seriously for a few hours. Bass, crappies, trout, bullheads, catfish, carp – all are plentiful and not too difficult to catch. Those needed for food are kept alive until required; the remainder returned to grow bigger. Ice-cold beer and cheese serve for lunch and, as progress is made down the lake, you realize that each bend, each bay, each cove in that vast desert water is a new adventure in its own right.

After a week you know you have only scratched the surface; that you would need years to explore just one small part of it. You realize that, in all that time, you have not seen or spoken to a single human being except the friends who have accompanied you, and you have not missed them at all. You have finally managed to 'get away from it all', and you know, deep down, that you will be back.

Those were my feelings when I left and I have indeed been back a number of times since.

In 1973 I went to Minneapolis by air, and then drove to Dent, Minnesota. Most of the little town's residents had already retired when I arrived and were sleeping soundly behind walls of roof-high drifted snow, and a full moon shone down out of a black sky putting a sparkle into the swirling snowdust on the road. It was intensely cold but I felt strangely warm inside.

Jack, my host, met me, looked at my open-necked attire and said, 'Hey, let's get out of here. The temperature's just hit zero and you're dressed for an afternoon picnic!'

It was, in fact, five degrees below zero Fahrenheit when I looked out next morning over Big MacDonald lake to where Jack's little insulated fishing house stood on some forty inches of snow-covered ice. This was my introduction to indoor and outdoor ice fishing for bluegills, crappies, walleye and tullibees. Tullibees I had never seen before. They are herring-like fishes of the Cisco family and make their under-the-ice spawning run in February. In water 100 feet or more deep, they can, with luck, be caught at varying depths.

Fishing through the ice calls for an attitude different from anything else I have ever experienced before and, naturally, the tackle is different too. Where depths in excess of fifteen feet are anticipated, a reel of some kind is necessary; in shallower water the line is put on to a line winder attached to the handle of a two-foot rod.

Jack had sited his fishing house in a spot where the water was some twenty feet deep and sealed it along the base line with soft snow. He had then drilled a double hole through the ice in readiness for our fishing. After breakfast we put on snow shoes and made our way out to it hauling a small sledge containing tackle, bucket, bait, power auger, ice-chisel and flasks of coffee. Ice had formed over the hole overnight but Jack tapped it out with the chisel and scooped it clear with an ice-ladle. Then two sticks of firewood in the tiny stove were lit and, within seconds, the temperature inside the house soared to over 70°F. The effect was quite amazing. Outside the air temperature was below zero, inside we were forced to remove our coats.

It was dark inside the house, of course, but the sun penetrated the snow and ice outside and lit up the fishing hole. Down eighteen feet our jigs and waxworms showed up in the gin-clear water. We worked them up and down slowly and watched for signs of fish. No floats were needed, we could see our baits and would know exactly what to do when bites came. In theory the jigs should have been sufficient in themselves, but Jack had learned that the added waxworm produced better bites.

It was quite fascinating. Dark shapes suddenly appeared in the bait area and the bluegills moved in to circle warily. One, braver than the rest, snatched at my slowly moving jig and I struck. It dived out of sight under the ice, but I handlined it back into view and teased it to the surface. When it was close to the hole I popped it clear and dropped it onto the hard-packed snow surface. Unhooked, it went into the paper-lined bucket and I began the tedious task of rewinding the loose line which was now spread over the floor of the house. My inexperience showed at once. Jack caught six more fish before I had another in the bucket, and these were handlined with care and precision. His spare line was confined to a small area between his feet and he was quickly back in business. I learned the trick eventually, and was probably taking one fish for every two of Jack's before we finally quit with thirty fish. They were not big, but bluegills are not noted for their size. They are highly regarded for their free biting, sporting and edible qualities. Our best might have weighed three-quarters of a pound but most were a little smaller. We took them back in a blaze of glory and three of us ate them all for tea! It would have been difficult to have eaten fresher fish than those.

That was the easy side of ice fishing. Next day it was different.

Jack and his friend Frank Waldiek decided that I ought to be ready for some outside fishing by then, and between them they hitched up the sledge behind the snowmobile. With Jack yelling 'mush' behind, I rode pillion dressed in ski suit, insulated boots, face mask and gauntlets. I was still half frozen before we reached our chosen spot which, to me, looked no different from anywhere else on that great expanse of ice. Jack and Frank fixed up the power auger, however, and began drilling holes several yards apart.

'This is a good perch spot,' said Frank. 'We'll use float tackle and fish about twelve feet deep.'

We had started out in sunshine but before long a cold wind caused the snow to swirl around our half-frozen feet. Great icicles formed on the floats as small perch after small perch came popping out through the ice. They stiffened on the crisp snow as the temperature continued to fall and, when the mercury finally reached 15°F below, and the wind chill factor had lowered it to equal 30°F below, we returned to base. I looked at those frozen perch and wondered if they felt any colder than my feet.

Frank's fishing house was a large affair. Sited at the beginning of winter it was to stay there, on the main tullibee run, until ice-out. Here the water was over eighty feet deep and tullibees had been taken fairly regularly at the fifty-to-sixty-foot level. His controlled gas heater kept the inside comfortably warm and rod-and-reel fishing was practical through the square holes cut in the ice at each corner. It was, in effect, touch ledgering, but with a difference. Our rods were about three feet long, our lines two-pound breaking strain and our leads comprised two swan-shots. At fifty feet the water was inky black. Delicate bites had to be felt on the finger tip and the fish, when hooked, had to be cranked to the surface. It was not quite as simple as it sounds, as some of them tipped the scales at over three pounds.

Outside a minor blizzard swirled. Inside we stripped to shirt-sleeve order and fished from our comfortable stools. I was undoubtedly outfished by my companions. My reactions to bites were too quick rather than too slow (a legacy from my years of experience in Britain) and it took me some time to recognize the problem. After a couple of days, however, I began to get the measure of those tullibees. I also got the taste for them; cooked in Frank's outdoor smoker, these rich, oily fish were truly delicious. So much so that Jack's wife Dorothy was obliged to tell me for my own good not to over-indulge.

These were our biggest fish. Some were taken from within the shelter of one or other fishing house; a few were taken in the open. The biggest fish we encountered, but unfortunately lost, was a wall-eye of about seven pounds that took Jack's jig one evening. Most evenings, just before dark, we would light two candles and set them on the edge of the ice hole. The heat from them was sufficient to keep us both comfortably warm in the confines of the small house, and so good was the insulation that, when fully clothed, we were often able to fish the evening stint without lighting up the stove at all.

It was just before candle time when the walleye appeared. I saw its great shape turn in the water, watched the jig disappear in its mouth and, from the corner of my eye, saw Jack's rod bend towards the ice. Then it was all over; the contest was too uneven. The line went slack and the walleye disappeared under the ice, probably unaware that it had been hooked.

We fished out in the open for crappies during the next few days and eventually, with borrowed snow boots, I managed to withstand the cold without too much discomfort. We popped enough fish through the ice to keep us well fed and somehow or other I managed to photograph some of our catch. Frank's big black labrador refused to enter the fishing house, but preferred to roll in the deep snow outside while we fished, and I never ceased to marvel at its stamina.

I fished one day with an old friend of Jack's, one Cecil Porter. He was of Indo-American descent, well over seventy and he fished or hunted most days. His little ice house was heated with an oil stove that belched smoke and almost suffocated us from time to time, and Cecil, his lower lip packed with a cud of chewing snuff or 'snoose', would swear at it. Then he would take to cursing me and finally the fish that refused to bite for most of the day.

'There must be a pike around,' he'd say. And he would fondle his great iron spear and add, 'I'll spike the son-of-a-bitch if I see it!' He never did, and I doubt really if he ever intended to. He was just being his 'natural ornery self'!

When I went to the United States in 1980, Cecil Porter took me to the Red River in North Dakota and said it was up to me to show him how to catch carp. His idea was to spear them on the spawning beds each year and I felt that he needed educating! He was quick to learn, and what is more, quick to appreciate the techniques involved. In the first hour he hauled a twelve-pounder ashore and almost did an Irish jig with delight.

'This one will go in the smoker,' he said. And fetched it a clout on the head! It is hardly an Englishman's idea of carp fishing but, when in Rome. . . . Smoked carp is delicious. You have my word for it!

Anyone who likes carp fishing and does not mind tackling fallen trees, beached branches and 'stick-ups' would have to enjoy the Red River. Stick-ups are tree tops poking out of the water and the spot I fished was full of them. They wash down with floods every year and naturally come to rest somewhere absolutely guaranteed to make fishing difficult. They remain there until the next spate moves them on again. Silt collects around the areas where they settle, and they become feeding grounds for monstrous carp. Streamlined, fast, common carp.

They are not as big as our own records, as many people seem to think, but they run up to about twenty pounds. It is tough but hilarious fishing. Once a big fish is hooked there is a chance that, by sheer pull-devil-pull-baker tactics (known there as 'horsing'), the snags can be avoided. Somehow a hooked carp helps the tackle ride over them; it is, I swear, impossible to retrieve and recast without losing tackle. But therein lies the fun.

Hooks have to be tough to handle big carp. Soft wire hooks would straighten and come free from the snags, but they would never hold a ten-pound carp. So, any attempt to fish is a compromise, and an acceptance of the fact that hooks will be lost. The trick lies in losing only the hook and not an expensive sinker as well. Sometimes, by using a separate hook link, it can be done; mostly a new hook is needed with each cast.

On that 1980 trip I had met Tom Opre in Detroit.

'Have you ever fished for muskies?' he asked me. 'If you fancy having a try we'll take off and fish with some guys I know in a lake that's supposed to hold plenty. It's a bit remote but I think I can find it.'

I had fished for muskies before, but never with any success, and I had a feeling on this trip that the time was still not yet ripe. Muskie waters are not common, and those that hold them are not often densely populated, but muskies stir the imagination. Legends have grown round these fish of the north. Tales have been told, and reputations have been won and lost. Muskies are lean and mean and savage. Muskies are mysterious and hard to catch. Muskies have broken tackle, hearts and even marriages in the past. No one who fishes for muskies on a casual, one-off basis is likely to succeed unless Lady Luck is in generous mood. I knew it from the start, but I had to try. And at the very beginning of the trial the rains came – such rains as are seldom seen in our own islands. Unceasing torrents drenched the roads, lightning bolts lit up the skies, thunder claps rattled above the big traveller, and an eerie daylight-darkness descended upon us as we travelled north over the Macinac to the Upper Peninsula.

The famous Au Sable River, where we broke our journey, was so far unaffected by the rain and, for a brief hour while the storm abated, we fished dry fly on this naturally stocked river. The trout in the main are small and there are stretches where it is said that they can be counted in thousands-per-mile. Here the brown trout take care of their own reproduction. Size limits are reversed and an angler may take five fish *below* a certain length and one *above* another. Those in-between sizes must be returned. Most anglers who fish the river with enthusiasm return all they catch anyway. Their pleasure lies in matching the hatch and placing their tiny dry flies with precision. Casting flies tied on no. 24 hooks is really beyond my capability, but I can appreciate the artistry involved and I was glad to have had the opportunity to fish.

Deep in the heart of the forest, on the edge of the secluded Upper Peninsula lake, we met 'the guys'. An old and one-time beautiful log-cabin lodge, now falling into disrepair, had been made available to us and the single gas lamp flickered as we tried to find our way to the rude but comfortable bunks. Outside the storm raged. Inside a great log fire began to roar as one of the group piled fresh dry logs on to the kindling, and soon the smell of hamburgers and coffee mingled with the pine log smoke. The muskie fishing would not materialize. I knew I would not rise at dawn to face the storm, launch a flimsy canoe and do battle with the elements. Let those who want to, do so, I counselled. And Tom grinned and said, 'You and me both, partner.'

But there were those who did. Call them dedicated or just plain crazy if you like. Anyone who ventures forth in a canoe at dawn on an exposed lake during an electric storm has to be one or the other; and my honest opinion is that it was the other. Especially without waterproofs!

Bacon, eggs, coffee and the warmth of the log fire suited the rest of us, and we stoked up in all respects until the lost souls and their canoe returned – fishless and half-drowned.

'The bird season opens in two days,' Tom reminded me. 'Should we not write this one off and see if we can do better hunting grouse?'

I had only ever hunted squirrels in the USA before, and I had never seen American bird dogs at work; but I had wanted to do so many times. I imagined it would be little different from our own walk-up shooting and that it would, of necessity, be a silent operation. But I found out two days later that I was so wrong!

Tom's bird dogs (English setters) and those of the other hunters who joined us, were fitted with bell collars and sent forward to hunt. The bells clanged in the distance, to the side and to the rear. The hunters moved forward in line into the thick woods chatting and calling to each other as they went. Each wore a fluorescent orange jacket with his state hunting licence pinned to the back, and there was no attempt made at concealment, camouflage or silence. It was a strange but exciting business.

I do not know how it is accomplished, but the American hunter knows his dog and the sound of its bell. When the bell stops ringing he knows that the dog is 'on point' and that it will stay thus until its owner arrives. Only then will the bird be flushed, and in the dense cover of the Michigan woods, the ruffed grouse offers but one fleeting second's opportunity. It is twenty-bore snap shooting of the highest standard and I saw some good shooting as well as some dismal misses. Birds I would never have considered possible to hit in the UK fell in the thicket and were retrieved by those remarkable dogs.

The sun shone, the woods had dried out, and there was a sweet 'mushroomy' smell rising from the ground. I walked and pushed my way through the dense growth trying hard to snap shoot with my camera, but eventually I knew it was not to be. Tom kept an exact count of the number of flushes and I believe it amounted to around fifty mixed woodcock and ruffed grouse. Of those, about twenty-five per cent were killed cleanly. Those birds were either dead or missed; I never saw a runner all day. I was impressed and

truly sorry when it ended, and I hope one day I shall return with my own gun to see if I can hold my own with those who hunt regularly in the great state of Michigan.

Minnesota is the home of the northern pike. I was fishing up there with Jack Vasconcellos and his neighbour's son Thaddeus. Jack swung the boat shoreward, cut the motor, and allowed the momentum to bring us to rest gently by the tie-up jetty.

Little ten-year-old Thaddeus was on the end looking at a broken line with eyes that were near to tears. 'A big fish broke my tackle and took my spoon,' he said. 'A big red and white daredevil spoon it was.'

He pointed. 'Right out there,' he said.

Jack and I winked knowingly to each other. Out there was a weed bed below the surface, and it was safe to assume that little Thaddeus had simply been 'weed busted'. The big fish was childish imagination.

It was right nevertheless that we should try to help him catch a fish to make up for his disappointment, and we rigged his tackle with a small red and white bobber float and a hook baited with a waxworm. At least we could make sure he caught some bluegills. We knew the weed bed was fairly crawling with these eager little biters.

One, two, three came skittering along the surface as the excited junior cranked them in, and then suddenly all bites ceased.

'Try over there to the right,' Jack instructed. And Thaddeus dropped the red and white bobber with a plop on the edge of the weed bed. As it touched, the water exploded and spray descended upon us on the jetty. Jack and I looked at each other, but this time there were no knowing winks. The most successful pike lure up there is the red and white daredevil spoon. The bobber had also been red and white. The bites from the bluegills had ceased and the monstrous swirl around the bobber had undoubtedly been caused by a northern pike.

'That's what happened before,' said little Thaddeus.

It marked the end of the fishing for that day. The bluegills retreated and refused to budge from their weedy sanctuary. The pike remained in charge but refused to be fooled by lures or baits of any kind until darkness fell.

Next morning I cast a black streamer fly to the edge of the weed bed as I had done every morning for a week previously. Morning is a good time, black streamers are good flies for bluegills, and I had taken my share daily.

The fly rod was almost pulled from my hand as I began a figure-of-eight retrieve, the water boiled, the reel screeched, and I was left with a bare line and a feeling of emptiness. The pike had struck again.

Suddenly I understood just how that little boy must have felt the day before when the big fish broke his tackle.

'Perhaps we're not as smart as we think,' I said to Jack later that day. 'Perhaps we can still learn something from kids.'

And Jack, one of the best fishers I have ever known, agreed.

'You'd better believe it!' he grinned.

9

Australian Interlude

I became a grandfather in 1973 and it didn't hurt a bit! I was sad, however, when my son-in-law and daughter decided to go to Australia, taking the light of my life, my lovely granddaughter, with them. A year or so later I could no longer resist the urge to visit them and booked a passage to Perth. I always had a yen to see the Australian countryside. Wild, hot, dusty and desolate places are not new to me and for some strange reason I enjoy them. My first impression of Western Australia was that there is a very large amount of it!

Only a few hours after touch-down I was already seeing and learning about bob-tailed goannas, racehorse lizards, red-backed spiders, kookaburras, and tiger snakes. Next morning I was up at dawn watching pelicans feeding, hawks hovering, and baby ducklings swimming around a vast freshwater lake. These were not set pieces, but wild creatures living naturally and seemingly undisturbed just a short distance into the bush.

The only kangaroo I saw during the first day was a tame one on the way from the airport, and as I always wanted to see one in the wild, I made up my mind to spend a great deal of time in the bush looking for them. I was keen to see a wild emu too and, of course, I began looking for rabbits the moment I arrived.

I took my fishing rods, hoping to enjoy some seasonable sport, but that was not to be. As far as I could gather, freshwater fishing simply did not exist within at least a 150-mile radius of Wanneroo. It's hard to imagine a freshwater lake without fish in it but I found myself almost surrounded by them and I was assured that there were hundreds more nearby. They were thick with tiny fry, but the fry of what? I tried to find out and identify them but could not do so. It was all very frustrating, especially when hundreds of fish-eating birds were seen to visit those lakes daily. In search of frogs, I was told. In the meantime, however, there was so much more to see in the way of flora and fauna entirely unique to Australia that I temporarily forgot about fishing.

The following morning I walked around the swampy side of Lake Joondalup, just looking and enjoying real space once more. Here and there, in a hundred different places, I discovered some tiny holes, big enough, perhaps, to accommodate a tennis ball. Around them all were the broken white shells of eggs about the size of that of a wood pigeon. Turtles of some kind or other, I guessed, and I recalled at once that marvellous film I'd seen on English television of those giant turtles elsewhere in the world.

The signs were that the hatchings had been recent and this was later confirmed by a regular visitor to the lake shores. They were not turtle eggs, I was told, but those of the long-necked swamp tortoise. The lake must hold countless thousands of these weird-looking creatures and rumour has it that an attempt to stock with carp some years ago was frustrated by their predatory habits.

'What on earth does a long-necked swamp tortoise look like?' I asked, a few days later.

'It's not so much what it looks like but what it smells like,' replied Ian, my son-in-law and host. 'But if you want to see one you shall.'

With a coarse fishing rod made up with a five-pound test line and a buoyant, bulky float, we tossed a strip of beef out into the lake. There was no hook attached. The meat was simply threaded on to the line with a needle and tied. Sitting there with a fishing rod on the banks of a fishless lake in the full heat of the midday Australian sun, we must have appeared completely crazy. Fortunately no one saw us – I hope!

Soon (and I'm convinced the presence of the meat strip drew them), small black heads began to appear briefly on the surface. The water rippled as one disappeared and another showed up nearby. I had not seen those heads before, and, while I realize that air breathers have to surface, I'm convinced that they must have done so previously in the shelter of the reed beds and tree stumps that cover vast areas of the lake. That, or our timing was exactly right by sheer coincidence.

The float dived under at that point and Ian gently bent the rod and began playing his catch. I sat with the big landing net in the water, utterly fascinated by the strength and aggression of the thing on the end. It had quite made up its mind that nothing was going to take that titbit away from it, and the more Ian bent into it, the harder it pulled. Eventually it came over the waiting net and I lifted it clear. I flatly refused to touch it, mainly because I reckoned its long neck would allow it to bite me irrespective of where I happened to be holding it; and remembering how the small, freshwater, snapping turtles in the USA can take off a man's finger, I stayed clear. Ian held it long enough for me to get a picture and a whiff of its disgusting smell. Then he tipped it back into the water.

At this stage we both began to wonder if there was any variation in size and if, in fact, there were such things as 'trophy tortoises'. Ian tossed the meat out again, the float dived under at once, and the procedure was repeated. Except that this time I took the net up the sandy bank and tipped the tortoise out to land on its back. Why anyone ever decided to call that creature a tortoise I shall never understand. Tortoises, as I know them, are slow and ponderous. This one was greased lightning! It righted itself and legged it back to the water at an amazing pace. The patch of yellow sand it had picked up on its back made it clearly visible in the water and Ian dropped the meat in its immediate path. Unbelievably it took it at once and allowed itself to be caught again. In all we caught that same tortoise four times before it learned that meat meant trouble!

During the next few days I wandered into the bush a number of times in the hope of spotting some of the larger creatures, but I saw only birds. Amazing birds. Birds I could not identify by sight or sound, birds that gave me immense pleasure. I saw, too, signs of kangaroo and wallaby, and, with help, positively discovered emu tracks and their drinking place. Ten million Aussie flies tormented me, otherwise I would have sat it out to watch for them all at evening time.

I also experienced becoming lost in the bush. Not hopelessly, but lost nevertheless. One gum, wattle, or 'black boy' tree looked very much like another to me, and my confusion arose out of the fact that directional sense differs entirely in the lower hemisphere. It was difficult, too, to understand a night sky with no north star, but, despite my confusion, there was a certain magic about these first few days that made me wish my trip would last for ever.

Meeting Ron Hoffner, as I did within a few days of arriving in Western Australia, was a remarkable stroke of luck. Ron had 1,600 acres of bush and swampland, six horses, six calves, several steers, two geese, some sheep and a bad-tempered old ram. He also had a sincere intent to turn the swamp into a watermelon, corn, and sweet potato patch, but I had the immediate feeling that it would never come about. There were, after all, a great many more important things to do on that untamed acreage. Like, for instance, building cabins, riding through the bush, spotting kangaroos, catching and breaking wild horses, watching emus, identifying birds, shooting rabbits, brewing bush tea and letting the world go by! I write these words years later, but I doubt if anything has changed.

Ron had origins in Sweden and was widely travelled; and although he spoke fair dinkum Aussie, a slight hint of Swedish accent crept in from time to time. He wore a bush hat, long-sleeved shirt, heavy jeans and leather boots; odd attire in an area where shorts and thongs were the dress of the day. Ron was wise in the ways of the bush, however, and knew well the effect of bites from tiger snakes, 'roo ticks, and other unpleasant little horrors. To have ignored his advice to dress in similar fashion when visiting his domain would have been both stupid and discourteous. I was, indeed, very glad of the jeans and footwear. They were essential for pushing through the thick brush we encountered when on Ron's walkabouts.

I believe I learned more about Australian wildlife in the short time I spent with him than I would have in a year on my own. What a mine of information he was; and what eyesight! He could spot a kangaroo at 200 yards in thick cover and shoot rabbits with an open sight .22 rifle at distances well in excess of 100 yards.

'I don't like shotguns,' he said. 'With the rifle I either kill or miss. I don't particularly care for rabbits but I hate the thought of wounding and losing one.'

When we talked of rabbits we were on common ground. Except that Ron knew nothing of long netting and other methods used in the UK. He understood a little about ferrets and ferreting but he was fascinated when, after he showed me the buries on his land, I explained a few of the inner mysteries of what goes on underground. Ron, for example, had seen bolt holes on occasions, but had not realized what they were. Understandably, he had regarded them as small cave-ins and not big enough to allow a rabbit to escape.

I was given the privilege of roaming at will over his terrain and had the opportunity of studying a great many rabbit buries. They were almost identical to our own 'sets' in soft sand, but strangely, there were very few bolt holes anywhere. Many were single-holed with no exit, which puzzled me at first but then I realized that perhaps Aussie rabbits have little need for escape holes. There are predators, but since most of those are hawks of one kind or another, any hole in the ground offers almost complete safety.

'Why don't you get hold of a ferret and come and catch yourself some?' asked Ron one day.

The January temperature at the time was 105°F – midsummer as near as made no difference – and I smiled tolerantly before explaining that no one uses ferrets in summer.

I should have known better of course! Summer, I learned, is the time when Australian rabbits are 'in season'. Their breeding ends when the hot weather arrives and there are no youngsters or pregnant adults around at that time.

I could well understand that the weather and conditions prevailing at that time were ideal for taking pot shots in the evening, and that is what I thought was in Ron's mind when he suggested Ian and I should join him for a rabbit hunt one evening. I expected that we would choose a likely spot, sit quietly and wait for an opportunity just before darkness fell. In fact, we walked the bush trails for miles, talking, watching birds, and other wildlife, until it was completely dark. As walking and talking did not improve out chances of a rifle shot, I was puzzled as to what Ron had had in mind. But I was to learn.

When it was completely dark we climbed into the car, switched on the scanner spotlight and went looking for our game.

I'd like to report that we came back with a sackful. I'd like to describe how we killed, dressed out, and barbecued a tender young doe in an open spit fire as was Ron's intention apparently. But on that first occasion we never made it. One rabbit showed up in the beam. It sat still while Ron climbed out of the car and shot. Unfortunately this was one of the few occasions when his hit-or-miss philosophy came into effect. 'Well, at least I missed it clean,' he said.

Many times I have chased English rabbits at night in a Land Rover. Many times I have walked them up with a rifle and powerful torch, but I have never hunted them over such shocking terrain, in a good quality saloon car. I have seen four-wheel-drives jib at some of the obstacles Ron negotiated in his totally abused motor car; but at least that explained why the exhaust had been fitted alongside rather than underneath.

Several times we worked those trails with nothing but bumps and bruises for our troubles before we finally quit, covered with sweat and sand. It was grey sand, made so by the charcoal from bush fires in previous years.

Ron was puzzled. 'I never fail to get a rabbit,' he said. 'In fact, all I ever bring down are the potatoes and onions!'

'That', I said, 'is known as "Sod's Law" in England!'

'But why tonight?' he asked.

'Do you normally walk round in the evenings before shooting?' I queried.

'No,' he replied. 'Never.'

'Then bear in mind the wise words of the old English farmer,' I said. I'd heard them over forty years ago and I knew them to be true. 'Always take a walk round the buries last thing at night if you want to keep your rabbits from long netters and other poachers,' he had said. I could only believe that it applied to Aussie rabbits too, and later experiences helped to prove it.

Ron had me up on horseback eventually. I had never ridden before and I certainly could not regard myself as particularly interested in horses, but with a Western saddle on a soft old horse that was used to being ridden Western style, I felt remarkably at ease. It was a great pleasure to follow the bush trails and watch from a high vantage point. Wild creatures seldom take fright at the sight of a horse, but bolt in panic at the sight of a human being on foot. Carrying a rifle and spotting rabbits from horseback was something entirely new to me and I felt a strange sense of control when old Jim responded to the slightest touch of the rein. I had, in my youth, driven cart horses and trap ponies. It was obviously necessary then to pull the left rein to turn left, and the right to turn right. Riding old Jim was different. The rein was simply flipped over to lie on the appropriate side of his neck. On the left, the loose-lying rein caused him to turn slightly left and vice versa. Strange to me; obvious perhaps to those who ride regularly and understand horses.

I never went at more than a walking pace. I couldn't. But I felt comfortable with old Jim, until Ron told me, 'He's too dumb to know you can't ride. If he did you'd be off in a second.' I was a little apprehensive after that!

Ron was the best rifle shot I ever knew. I never saw head shots so cleanly executed, and I noticed that he was able to use his left shoulder and left eye just as well as his right. I do not pretend to understand how he managed it. I always imagined that the master eye was the only one to be used for accurate rifle shooting, but I learned differently in the bush. I could never hope to shoot as well, nor did I have the ability to spot rabbits on the edge of the beam as he did. He was his own biggest critic, however, and having brought off what I considered a fantastic shot, he invariably looked at the carcase to see exactly where his bullet had hit. He used hard-hitting, copper-coated bullets, and there can be no doubt that head shots are essential with such ammunition. I remember a shot, taken from the left shoulder, that splintered the rabbit's neck and killed it instantly. When I congratulated him on an excellent shot, he was not in the least impressed. 'It was *not* a good shot,' he said. 'I aimed for its head!' And he meant it. I would like to think that I could have been as particular myself, but I never could. There was no way I could compete with someone able to pick out a pair of kangaroo's ears at 200 yards and spot an emu's foot among the dense bush foliage fifty yards distant.

I could compete with him in the field of outdoor cooking, however, and, despite his years of bush experience, I believe he preferred me to prepare the meals we shared. I never presumed to take over the task of making billy tea, because I felt sure I would get that part wrong. The smoky old billy, with a burn-hole in the side, had to be brought to the boil. The carefully and accurately measured handful of tea was dropped in and allowed to bubble for a minute or so. Then the billy was removed and the whole boiling mass swung around in a complete circle at arm's length. Magically the leaves all settled on the bottom; the tea was brewed. I took it black with neither milk nor sugar and, in a land where most people preferred cold beer, I found it the most refreshing drink of all. It was an outdoor drink, of course; no indoor stove could impart that real smoky bush flavour. My steaks, my eggs and bacon, my barbecued rabbit, were eaten with enthusiasm, and often we talked on long after we should have been doing other jobs. But that was my short apprenticeship, my real introduction to life in the bush. I remained completely turned around, often hopelessly lost by day and night, in that southern hemisphere and for that reason I seldom ventured far alone. My rabbit hunting had to be carried out with someone who knew the way and I could not have asked for a better guide and companion than Ron Hoffner. I met Ernie Chitty a short time later, however, and my education continued.

*   *   *

If anyone had told me I'd be running around at midnight in January, dressed in bedroom slippers and swimming trunks trying to catch rabbits with my bare hands, I'd have said he was crazy. But you have my word for it – that's how it was.

Ernie Chitty, landowner, naturalist and superb horseman, promised Ian and me that he would take us one evening for a session of 'roo spotting followed by an hour or two's rabbit spotting. There is a difference. 'Roo spotting is a gentle pastime indulged in by many Australians. It's akin to bird watching in so far as the object is to watch kangaroos feeding at close quarters from a concealed vantage point. Rabbit spotting generally means shooting rabbits in the beam of a powerful spotlight after dark.

At that time, when parts of the UK were being pounded by gales, floods and blizzards, Perth was experiencing the heatwave to end all heatwaves. The mercury finally peaked at 44.7°C – the highest ever recorded in the city's history. Farther north in the bush where I was hiding out for a few days, it was over 2°C higher. In my language that's around 116°F, and in any language that is *hot*. However, while the Aussies wilted and whinged, this old ex-Desert Rat lapped up every glorious moment of it. I brewed billy tea, cooked bacon over an open fire and revelled in the freedom of it all. Mad dogs and Englishmen. . . .

With the bushland a veritable tinderbox, however, it is not surprising that Ernie became involved in fighting some very tough bush fires. For two days and nights, along with willing helpers, he rode on horseback and pick-up truck to backburn and rescue his stock – which included fifty valuable horses. When I saw him, fire blackened and exhausted, being interviewed on television, I realized that the 'roo and rabbit spotting simply wasn't on.

But Ernie told me on the phone later that night that we'd manage it one way or another.

'No worries, mate,' he said. 'A promise is a promise; give us another day and she'll be right.'

And right she was!

The 'roo spotting was not a wild success. We saw none where we had planned, but several crossed the track at a distant point. It was a great and pleasurable experience for me, but for some reason these sensitive animals decided not to venture closer on that particular evening. Perhaps the smell of that distant fire smoke had made them over-cautious. We'll never know.

Back in Ernie's tack room we dug out the .22 automatic rifle, fixed up the powerful spotlight, climbed aboard the four-wheel-drive 'ute' (Aussie for utility pick-up truck) and set out into the dark bushland. Ernie took the wheel, Ian took the spotlight and I took the rifle (because it was thrust upon me). On the back of that bouncing open truck, still bearing the scars of its recent encounter with the bush fires, I found difficulty in staying in one spot for more than a second at a time. What I'd do if and when my chance to shoot came I could not conceive. But it was an exhilarating ride if nothing else.

Several rabbits hopped off in the distance and disappeared. Ernie gunned the motor and I have a vague recollection of coming to a sudden stop against the front cab as a rabbit appeared in the spot. Ernie held the vehicle still, Ian held the light steady and I suppose I must have done the same with the rifle. There was a soft 'thwack' as I squeezed the trigger, the rabbit dropped and never moved again. A perfect head shot; and Ernie gave me full credit as I chucked it in the back. 'Not a bad start for a Pom,' he chuckled.

A few minutes later I executed a precise repeat and picked up number two. At this point I decided it might be wise to quit while I was still ahead. I'd an idea that a certain amount of luck had been involved, despite the obvious accuracy of the weapon! So I took the spot; Ian took the rifle. He missed a couple but quickly put matters right by making two consecutive clean kills immediately afterwards. I took the rifle again, missed two good shots because I was overconfident and finally took care of number five. Another head shot.

Ernie pulled into the clearing where his wind-pump was clanking merrily in the breeze and producing a nonstop stream of water from the depths of that arid land. Burning tree trunks, fanned by the breeze, glowed in the distance, but Ernie assured us that they would simply burn themselves out on that already charred acreage.

In the headlights of the 'ute' I gutted the rabbits, buried the entrails and washed up in the water from the pump. Those five prime rabbits, good food, fat as butter despite the near-desert conditions, were, I decided, sufficient for our needs. None would be wasted but I felt that there was no point in killing more, and I declared that enough was enough.

Ernie agreed. 'We'll keep one up the spout in the rifle in case we see a fox,' he said. 'But on the way back we'll see if we can bamboozle a few rabbits and catch 'em by hand.'

The night was warm, and I was, as already mentioned, dressed only in swimming trunks and slippers. The slippers were to protect my bare feet against stones, thorns and possible snakes, but in the end I suppose I did more chasing barefooted than I did fully shod.

If you think shooting rabbits at night is fun; if you enjoy long-netting in complete darkness; you should try making rugby tackles at Australian bush rabbits. That, my friends, can only be described as hilarious!

The rabbits are confused; the odds are reduced a little as the light sweeps across the horizon and the motor roars in the darkness, but only when the light shines directly into their eyes does the hunter really have a chance.

'Keep the spot on 'em all the time, Fred,' yelled Ernie, 'and we'll surround the blighters and make 'em surrender.' How many we chased up steep slopes only to lose down convenient holes I couldn't begin to remember. How many I touched but failed to hold on to as they crashed into thorny bushes I've no idea. What those poor rabbits made of it all is anyone's guess. But finally we nailed one. It travelled up the beam towards me slowly, uncertainly, and completely bewildered. Ian grabbed it; Ernie dispatched it and that, we said in unison, was that.

With the daylight, I skinned, washed and portioned the rabbits, covered them completely with ice cubes and let the flesh set firm. That night we ate an Aussie rabbit tea and, as I looked at the meagre pile of bones that remained, I marvelled at how good and sweet it had tasted.

Rabbits are not rated highly in Western Austrlia, but despite the difference in the food they eat, the land on which they live, and the temperature they have to endure, I have to admit that they're equal to our own. Perhaps even a little better.

There was an emptiness in my life, it seemed, when I returned from Australia. I had spent the Christmas period trying to teach my granddaughter to swim. She, who had fallen into deep water twice previously and been hauled out in a state of terror, was not easy to convince. 'I've been drownded twice already,' she informed me quite seriously. It took time and patience, but there was a successful end result. She now swims like a fish.

Having a million miles of space to share with a million Western Australians was like a dream come true. Having a whole beach to myself in the mornings, soaking up sunshine, eating massive barbecued steaks for dinner, shooting rabbits, watching birds, bush walking, exploring, fishing, body surfing and 'bumming around' in shorts with no worries of any kind was fantastic. I knew then that I had been right all those years ago to decide to live modestly in a closing-in situation so that I might be able to afford the luxury of travelling to those wild and lonely places I loved so much. But it made me discontent. I longed to return there and to those other desolate areas of desert, bush, mountain and wilderness I had visited and revisited over the years. I had crossed the Atlantic and back almost every year since 1967. Some years I had crossed it twice. I had fished in twenty-six of the United States of America and I had revelled in the bush and timber country of Canada. On every occasion the vastness of the countries I had visited enthralled me and I was, suddenly, discontent.

I thought that as I grew older I would have to work harder and longer for less and less and pay more and more taxes to keep some of the layabouts who sought to stop me from practising my legitimate sports. I knew that some of those who opposed my beliefs were sincere, but I had, and still have, no time for those who are not sincere, who have no respect or feelings for the creatures concerned, and who are ever ready to prey upon me and others like me for their existence. I did not believe then, nor do I believe now, that I should contribute to their welfare. I thought there was a freedom in Canada, America and Australia that was missing from our own green and pleasant land, and I began seriously to think of going back to Australia to live.

In the meantime, however, I received some remarkable news from Florida:

   I had not planned to go to the United States that particular year,
and indeed I began thinking about who could take my place to collect the award. I never found out who nominated me, nor do I
know, to this day, why I was so chosen. Certainly it was not for
expertise. It was explained to me, very precisely, that in the event
that the choice should lie between an expert angler and a conservationist, the expert would be less likely to be accepted. I could only
find out that I had been accepted for 'several good reasons' and that
everyone hoped I would be able to attend in person. Eventually my
family persuaded me that I should go, and since I really wanted to
visit the AFTMA tackle show in Atlanta, Georgia, I packed my bags
and went.
   It was an emotional moment for me to step up to the rostrum and
accept my award, and it was a great pleasure to talk to General Mark
Clark afterwards. Several of my American friends attended the
ceremony and I was glad of their support at this rather splendid
occasion.
   The Silver Dolphin Award now hangs in the hallway of my small

bungalow, alongside a tench engraving by the late David Carl-Forbes, which is inscribed 'To the best Tenchman of our time'. I am very proud of them both.

I came back from the USA after collecting my award and visiting as many of my American friends as possible in the few weeks I spent there. I fished with Jack Vasconcellos in Minnesota, Tom Opre and Bing McClellan in Michigan, Jack Ehresman in Illinois, Judge Thresher in Arkansas and Tryg Lund in the timber country north of Wawa in Ontario, Canada. Tryg had driven almost non-stop from Atlanta, Georgia to Wawa – a distance of around 1400 miles. There we had pitched camp and fished waters, some of which had almost certainly never been fished before. It was an adventurous trip and very exciting for me, but I was utterly exhausted when I returned to England.

By the following October, however, Carrie and I had sold up and were on our way to a new life in Australia.

I thought that I was smart enough to opt out of the 'rat race', to set up a new home near to my loved ones, and to enjoy a life free from the pressures of business. I had a small income and sufficient capital to purchase a home with a big wild and unkempt garden and a fair-sized swimming pool. I bought a hard-topped Land-Rover and used it to explore the nearby bush land and to come to terms with the West Australian environment. I planned to cross the Australian continent and write up my experiences in book form when I learned enough of that vast country to feel confident that I could do so without unnecessary risk.

It was approaching high summer when we arrived, and I revelled in the sunshine, knowing from past experience that each day would be much the same as the next, and that the temperature could rise to the 40°C mark eventually. It was truly wonderful to rise every morning and dive into my own pool to start the day, and for a while there was much to occupy my time. A 40°C temperature is not con-ducive to gardening or shed-building, or the many other outdoor tasks that I found to be essential, but I stuck with them and began to see results in the shape of improvements to the pool, surrounds and entrance to my home. All the time, however, I was longing to hunt, and my thoughts were always with the outdoor life of Australia and what it had to offer.

I retrieved my guns from Customs, acquired a full Australian driving licence, resumed work on the third edition of my first book, *Angling in Earnest*, and, for the first time, began to make comparisons seriously.

There, in the state of Western Australia, where summer sun and drought had quickly changed green to brown, where bush fires raged and hazard notices remained on 'high', and where the inhabitants were referred to as 'sandgropers', I realized that life would be different from what I had imagined. I had never expected it to be easy, and I knew many of the problems I would have to face. I knew my hunting and fishing would be different and that despite predation comprising foxes, dingoes, wild cats and eagles, there were rabbits a-plenty for me to hunt. Despite the tales told about Australian infestations, however, there did not appear to be the same number of rabbits per acre as are present in the UK. There were no signs of bodies on the road during the early mornings, and it was unusual to see rabbits hopping about during the daylight hours. Occasionally, when walking through the bush, one would show for a fleeting moment and disappear into cover, but there was little chance of approaching a sighted rabbit for a shot. Usually the sighting came as a complete surprise, with the rabbit and me being equally startled.

Like their UK counterparts, Western Australian rabbits are very nocturnal and the fact that very few seemed to be killed on the roads was puzzling. I recalled that when I was making regular trips to Hampshire's River Test it was not at all unusual to see forty or fifty dead bodies along the ninety-mile route. When large numbers of young rabbits were present, those figures might well have been doubled, and it was my practice often to pick up half a dozen of the less-mangled carcases for ferret food.

On reflection, of course, since these bush roads probably carry but one car for every hundred or so carried by similar UK roads, the slaughter could well be proportional. When other motorists began flashing their lights at me on lonely bush roads I wondered what could be wrong. I learned later that their drivers were simply greeting another road user; probably the first they had seen for an hour or so! That, I thought, would almost certainly explain the lack of road-killed rabbits.

When mention was made of rabbit shooting, the main topics were usually concerned with spotlights and rifles. The most popular way of shooting was almost invariably from the back of a four-wheel-drive truck after dark. It was not my idea of the most civilized way of shooting, but it was enjoyable, exciting and effective.

My 200,000 candle-power spot was put to use very effectively and because, unlike many other lights, it did not have the central 'dead spot', it picked up and held at a much longer range. In fact, I realized there was often no need for the rifle at all. If the 'lamp man' held steady and kept the illuminated rabbit in the centre of the beam, it was fairly easy to pick it up by hand. Some dexterity was needed and there was often a certain amount of diving and grabbing handfuls of sand (sandgroping in fact) but, if the spot was kept on the rabbit, it seldom managed to leave the lit-up area.

To this day I recall the aches and pains I suffered as a result of hanging on to a pick-up roof while travelling over rough terrain at about forty m.p.h. With one hand holding the rifle and only one hand holding on, it is a miracle I am here to tell the tale. But there are no means of communication between shooter and driver, and if the driver happens to be Ernie Chitty, and the light is on a pair of foxes, it really becomes a survival exercise. How well I recall the night when the spot picked up two pairs of eyes in the distance and suddenly the steady trundling of the vehicle turned into something akin to an after-dark chariot race.

'Foxes,' yelled Ernie, and we left the ground at the precise moment. 'Shoot the blighters, shoot the blighters,' he bellowed and the truck took off once more. At thirty yards' range both foxes were confused and the truck slowed momentarily. I took aim to shoot, the foxes moved on, and Ernie gunned the motor again. My shot was probably three feet off target; so too were the several others I fired. I never did learn how to hold on with one hand and fire a rifle accurately with the other while my feet were hanging in midair. We lost sight of the foxes when an enormous cat ran directly into the beam. That cat was at full stretch and covering ground at an incredible rate. It appeared to be as big as a cougar, and if I had been told that cougars were present, I would have believed this to be one. It has been said that American sailors left all kinds of weird mascots behind during the war years and many still believe that some of the

big cats spotted in wild country are their offspring. But it seems that feral cats grow to huge proportions in the bush and Ernie, commenting that it was unusually large, confirmed that 'our' cat was nothing more than that. He is a stock farmer and it would appear that his three pet hates are cats, dingoes and foxes – in that order. Seeing the cat put all thoughts of the two foxes out of his mind. Priorities changed, but the end results were the same. More body pounding and more missed shots.

The well-worn tracks of that 3000-acre farm were not new to me. I never got to know them all, but I travelled them a number of times. Each time I was petrified at the sight of enormous spiders' webs looming up at face level in the darkness. In their centres were large spiders (bigger by far at night than by day), and I ducked, sometimes too late, to avoid being enmeshed with something like heavy-duty candyfloss. The feeling was one of disgust and fear, particularly if the whereabouts of the spider itself remained unknown. These spiders were harmless but, because they were often called tarantulas (rightly or wrongly), they gave me the horrors.

On one exceptionally dark night about a hundred kangaroos and bush wallabies showed in the beam. Once lit up they made little attempt to move and it was easy then to understand how the old 'roo hunters were able to fill a truck with carcases overnight. It is said that some still practise 'roo shooting for sport, but I found it hard to understand how a sporting aspect could present itself. These timid and rather special creatures were utterly helpless in the beam of the powerful lamp.

Tiny groundlarks (strictly pipits I believe) rose in dozens in front of us as we journeyed home by the roundabout route on one occasion. They presented yet another aspect of the bush I had not seen before. They looked to be almost like large moths in the powerful light, and I was utterly fascinated by their short flights to safety and their quick return to the ground once the beam had been cleared. I was of the opinion that these were the smallest birds I had ever seen (smaller even than humming birds I thought) but since the reference book lists them as sixteen centimetres long I can only assume that the light played tricks with my eyes.

Australian rabbit hunting was indeed different from anything else I had tried. It is true that I had used spotlamps in England to hunt them at night, but those operations had mostly been carried out during the wild nights of winter. I could never get used to having to dress out my rabbits while they were still warm, but I became quite adept at keeping them in excelent condition for the table.

Geoff Southern and Phil Green picked me up at 6 a.m. the first time I went ferreting Aussie fashion. I wore swimming trunks and a tee shirt, and carried a gallon of iced water as my only sustenance. In a temperature of 100°F liquid is more important than food.

We unloaded the gear after a sixty-mile drive, and gave the ferrets a drink before setting the first bury. It was an odd situation – different in so many respects but exciting nonetheless. June, Geoff's wife, came along too – as keen and as efficient as any man – and I was pleased to note that all three spoke in whispers as we worked.

The nets were regular purse nets, made by Geoff out of strong twine, and were carried hanging loose on a big retaining ring. Pegs, because of the hard nature of that near-desert terrain, were made of iron! They had to be 'worked' into the ground and the nets were simply looped over them.

Any rabbits caught were *not* killed but put alive into a large wire cage or a sack to be dispatched later. If dispatched at once they would have been 'high and fly blown' in a matter of minutes.

Extracting a live rabbit from a purse net was not new to me, but I had to check myself several times as my instinct is to dispatch rabbits at once while they're still in the net. By 10.30 a.m. it was over. The merciless sun was making the ground almost too hot to walk on, and the ferrets, finding comfort in the dark, cool, underground tunnels, were beginning to show reluctance to come out. We picked up, dressed out the rabbits, and made for home and a long, cold beer!

I have often said that every ferreting situation is different. This one surely was. I refer to it to this day as the first time I ever tried my hand at bikini ferreting!

Once when Ron Hoffner and I were bush walking, he pointed out a tiger snake's tracks. 'It went this way,' he said. 'Let's follow it. I'll go first; then if I disturb it, it will bite you and not me.'

I *think* he was joking.

We had hardly walked ten yards when we were confronted. The snake was about forty inches long and, after a second's hesitation, it moved off ahead at a remarkable pace. I have seen some brilliant shooting in my time but never have I seen a shot like the one Ron made then. He swung the .22 like a shotgun and the bullet cut the snake cleanly into two pieces. Unfortunately the head end was longer than the tail end and, although the snake was obviously doomed, it turned to the attack. Ron stepped on it and the last I saw of its head was when it disappeared up the inside of his jeans! Fortunately he was, as always, wearing high boots. 'Where's its head?' he asked. 'A foot or so up your trouser leg,' I yelled.

I was in no danger at all, but I was scared stiff for Ron. Apart from not knowing what action to take, I could not imagine myself being able to carry him out of the bush should it have become necessary.

He just grinned. 'I can see his bottom part,' he said. 'He can't get past the top of my boot.' And to prove it he rolled up the leg of his jeans. The snake had taken hold of the leather about an inch from the boot top and it was undoubtedly not playing games. Eventually it released its hold and Ron stamped it into the ground.

That was my first encounter with a tiger snake. I had heard of them and I had decided to respect them and keep a sharp eye open for them. But proof of just how easy it is to step on one came a couple of days later when I walked through a fairly open stretch of bushland around noontime. Before I could stop myself, I had placed my foot on a tiger snake lying across the narrow track. Its markings were unmistakable; my reaction was immediate. Scared out of my wits I jumped and fled and, with a pounding heart, turned around to see where the snake was. It was still there. Or at least the discarded skin of what I had believed to be a real tiger snake was still there! I can chuckle about it now, but it was *not* funny at the time. And I had once walked in the bush in shorts and sneakers, confident that I could see any snake in my path. That little episode fully convinced me that I could not!

A fox, too, taught me a lesson. Thirty-five chickens, four bantams and one goose disappeared in three nights from Ron's farm, and the maze of tracks left no doubt as to the identity of the culprit (or possibly culprits). But there were so many tracks it was difficult to work out the direction they had taken. Ron watched silently through several nights, rifle in hand, ready to deal with the midnight marauder, but it seemed he (or she) always arrived on the scene at about 6 a.m.; each time by a different route, and each time out of range.

We followed a set of clear prints once but lost the trail when it petered out into a dusty nothingness. Off the trail, and well into cover, Ron showed me a pot hole or cave which might have made a good retreat or lair, but a cobweb across the small entrance indicated that it had not been used recently. I would not venture into the cave without a torch, but when, at Ron's suggestion, I hung my arm inside I felt a cold breeze. 'There must be another entrance,' he said. 'If we could find it we might find the fox or foxes, but it could be half a mile or more away, of course.'

There were no signs in the blackness to point the way and, although Ron himself ventured into the cavern, he was unable to locate another way out. The clearing in front of it looked to be an ideal stake-out spot, however, and we decided to pitch a tent on the high ridge above; to be ready and waiting with the dawn – and a loaded rifle. Ron put up the tent and let it remain there untouched for several days so that it would become part of the general scenery and not be looked upon with suspicion.

On the third day he told me excitedly that he had located the lair and possibly the other entrance to the cave. Under a limestone overhang, tucked away in the brush, was another dark hole.

Outside, the ground was littered with the bones of chicken and rabbit. A whole goose skeleton told the rest of the story.

A quick survey showed there were several 'runs' away from the main entrance, but all seemed to join up with the main trail eventually. The clearing where we had prepared our stake-out was part of the route and we set to work breaking off twigs, bending down saplings and clearing the way for an unobstructed shot. We would probably only get one chance and would have to make it count. That night I took two rabbits, pierced their stomachs, dragged them along the trail from the lair to the clearing and left them there as bait. Ron and I crawled into our sleeping bags and talked quietly as we peered over the ledge to where the bait lay.

A full moon lit up the area like a spotlight. We, on the ledge, were in pitch darkness; the clearing was as light as day. The night grew cold, our whispered conversation slowed down and eventually stopped altogether as we crawled deeper into the warmth. Soon we were asleep. I was only awakened once by the hooting of an owl and the replies of another in the distance. It was irritating at the outset, but soon I put myself 'in rhythm' with their calls and drifted off again.

I awoke with the dawn, opened one eye and saw Ron reaching for the rifle. It was cold, but I eased myself out and reached for the camera just in case.

It took about two seconds to discover that the rabbits were no longer where they had been left. The bait had been taken, but the trap had not been sprung. The fox had fooled us both and, on reflection, that was really no more than we deserved. It was not very smart to leave two fox-sized meals a few yards from the lair and expect them to be left strictly alone until dawn. Notwithstanding those regular morning excursions, the fox had obviously done much of its hunting by night and had probably been on its way home when spotted previously. We should have remembered, but we were too full of our own ideas to consider failure.

It was, however, a good lesson to learn. I could have snared the fox easily; but there were horses and other animals to consider. Obviously with a pinch of the right sort of powder, I could have put paid to it once and for all now that I knew where to put the bait, but, although I had no love for that fox, I believe it warranted a better end.

We tried several more times to come to grips with the midnight marauder but always it escaped or avoided our traps, and shortly afterwards all signs of it disappeared. We thought perhaps the vixen had reared her cubs in what had been good hunting territory at the time and had moved on elsewhere once they were big enough to travel. We never saw signs of it again but Ron and I spent much more time in the bush together. Sitting around the fire, cooking rabbits or huge steaks over the embers, and talking into the early hours was part of the good side of life in Western Australia. I will always remember those golden days and nights. But somehow it did not last. I had no challenge. I did not have to scheme or work hard for those pleasures. I had new friends, but I missed the old ones. I had no real problems and yet those I had were magnified. I missed the rush hours, the deadlines and the rat race, and I learned, sadly, that despite the great feeling of freedom portrayed by its wide open spaces, Western Australia was not the land of true freedom I had hoped for. There is a great cameraderie among its peoples, but I saw it as a somewhat selfish land where only the strong and the ruthless were likely to survive. I fought with the Aussies in Tobruk and I will not say or listen to a bad word about them for that reason; but, probably quite wrongly, I saw their laws and taxes as unreasonable.

It was my own fault entirely; I should not have hastened to the other side of the world, and I should have listened. . . .

My frustrations brought upon me a strange depression which was completely alien to my nature and for which there was no real reason. It became worse daily. Perhaps there is no joy to be achieved from having everything and wanting for nothing. For a while I had revelled in my supposedly new-found freedom and, despite the sadness, I would never deny that Western Australia held – and still holds – many treasured memories for me; but I now know that my roots had been planted too deeply in England.

10
The Changing Scene

I came back from the sand and heat of Western Australia to the ice and snow of Buckinghamshire on my birthday in February 1979. I had both business and personal problems to attend to and there was good reason for my journey. But, looking back on the events, I doubt very much if I ever intended to use the return half of my airline ticket. I had allowed for three weeks, during which time I could, perhaps, indulge in some ferreting, pigeon shooting, and a little pike fishing to end the season. It all went sour on me from the beginning. The fields and hedgerows were buried under a blanket of snow and, while I am prepared to tackle most ferreting situations, I jibbed at this one. It had been 100°F when I left Perth; the change was too much.

My pigeon-shooting friends told me there was no sport left. The half-starved birds were too easy and not worth the effort. I had a few shots and I found myself in agreement. It was not for me. Those pathetic birds, with breast bones like ice skates, could never be allowed to grace my table. And, as I simply do not enjoy shooting what I cannot eat, I cleaned and put away my gun.

I should have known, of course, that it was a waste of time reaching for my pike rod. Every water near to hand was frozen over and fishing was out of the question. I have fished through ice many times before. I have, in fact, fished through forty inches of it in northern Minnesota, but there I was dressed for the part. Here I had neither the means nor the courage to drill a 'fish hole'.

After a few days the snow began slowly to disappear. Crisp frosty mornings followed which, though they made driving difficult, made walking the fields a pleasure. I had shot as many rabbits as I needed in Western Australia but I could never heartily indulge in what is commonly referred to in the UK as a 'walk round'. The heat during the day made the going too tough. It was better to sit and wait with a rifle or to use a spotlight at night. Either required less effort and offered better opportunity.

'Walk rounds' had been part of my life for so many years, however, that I missed them. It felt good to be negotiating fences and gates again, even if it was strange to be wearing boots after so many months of running barefoot, or at best wearing a pair of 'thongs' or 'flip flops'. But when I disturbed a hare, my first chance of the day and a perfect going away shot, I may have been daydreaming, or simply enjoying the air, but I did not raise the gun. I was confused. I had been turned around for so long and so involved with strange 'seasons' that it somehow seemed wrong to shoot. Perhaps the hare reminded me of the wallabies I had occasionally disturbed during my bush walks in Australia but, whatever the reason, the chance had long gone by the time I had collected my wits.

It was, I recall, 24 February, and I walked on thinking that soon it would be mad-March-hare time again. I stopped at the gate where the hare had disappeared, sat on a stump, poured a cup of coffee from the flask and looked across the next big meadow. The sun was melting the frost on the big barn roof; the hedgerow, still shaded, was white with hoar frost. I moved around to the warmer side, dragged out a bale of straw and sat, cold hands clasped round the second steaming cup. It should have been a morning full of life but, strangely, nothing moved. Even the song birds were silent. I had no dog but it is doubtful if I would have fared any better with one. The hare had only moved because I had almost kicked it and I resigned myself to a blank walk round. The countryside remained silent and still.

I put my finger to my mouth and 'squawked'. Just for fun. I do it at some time or other most days when I am out in the fields, with or without a gun. Usually it fails to do more than echo back, but there are days when it brings hares from distant fields. In Australia it occasionally stopped rabbits dead in their tracks despite the fact that they were running from a moving truck and a spotlight.

Today I wondered, with little optimism, if it would bring back the hare I had disturbed earlier, and I was totally unprepared for what happened. Silently and unhurriedly, the red shape of a fox, showing up against the white hedge background, padded up the gentle slope towards me. I sat completely still and squawked again. The fox stopped, listened, and continued its leisurely approach. I was not concealed and I can only believe that, against the dark background of the barn, my outline was broken. The fox came to within ten paces of me (I stepped them out later), stopped and looked straight at me. It did not seem interested or puzzled or in any way concerned. Was it a day when the scent was bad? I'll never know the answer because, as is my crazy custom in these situations, I spoke quietly to it. 'Hello fox,' I said.

Its reaction was incredible. Jumping, and literally turning at right angles in the air, it hurled itself at a gap in the hedge and disappeared. Had I wished to shoot it as it approached, I could have done so easily, but if I had any ideas of taking a 'sporting shot' I would never have made it. The fox was gone long before I could have closed my gun.

That day, as I returned to base with nothing to show for my efforts, I made the decision to stay in the UK. I think I realized then that I was ill and that I could not resolve the problem from the other side of the world. My stay in paradise had been short and I was truly sad in many ways to leave it. But there was a feeling of gladness too. I had to start all over again; the challenge was back.

I was always interested in the Game Fair, the event organized annually by the Country Landowners' Association, and I once reported in my 'Countryman' column in *Shooting Times and Country Magazine* that the highlight of the whole show for me had been a close-up view of a particularly magnificent hawk. It had been carried around for the purpose of promoting some good cause or other, and I had spent some time admiring it. I wrote that I had never been involved in the hawking scene, that I envied those who were, and that I was greatly disappointed in not having been able to see the falconry display.

The outcome of those remarks resulted, through the good offices of one Walter Pipe, in my being invited up to Lichfield for the International Meet organized by the Welsh Hawking Club in 1979. I travelled up with Walter in the late afternoon and we were welcomed in the evening by the President, Lorant de Bastyai.

The following day dawned dull but dry, and I duly visited the farm buildings where the hawks were housed. Beautiful birds they were, a great host of them. I had little idea of their species, except that I recognized the kestrels, and I could hardly have been mistaken about the magnificent eagle that seemed quite unconcerned about the whole procedure. But one bird in particular attracted me. I looked through the wire and wondered. Could it be? The voice of John Buckner behind me brought me back to reality. 'Yes, Fred,' he said. 'That is the very one you admired at the Game Fair.' She was, he said, his own Harris's hawk, being flown that day by Laurie Workman. Her name was Harriet, having been hastily changed from Harry when certain biological facts had come to light. There were three others of the same breed present, all belonging to John and another hawker, Ceri Griffiths. If anyone had asked me to pick Harriet out of the bunch together, I could not have done so. They were all superb creatures, and yet somehow I had known.

'We shall break up into four parties today,' said John, treasurer of

the Association. 'If you want to see what your bird can do in the field, why not come along with us for the day?'

There was nothing I wanted more and, after the meet had been declared open by Mr Van Nie, President of the Dutch Falconry Club, I moved off with John, Laurie, Griff and a few overseas guests, two English springers, two short-haired pointers, and a band of followers. My absolute ignorance of hawking must have been a source of annoyance to the experienced. My nonstop questions probably made them wish I'd stayed at home, and yet they suffered me, if not gladly, at least with tolerance.

I had not known of the intimacy of hawking. My complete knowledge of the subject revolved around some television programme involving, I believe, peregrine falcons. That programme filled me with admiration for the birds, but it had led me to believe that this was the way of all hawking. Miles of space, open country, an unlimited bank balance, and a certain remoteness from the birds involved seemed to be necessary, and there was no way that I, a humble rabbiter, could ever become involved. Which simply goes to prove how wrong a man can be. It is a much more intimate sport than I at first believed, and I felt that John put a name to it when he suggested it was akin to rough shooting without guns. I could not have put it better.

The dogs worked the rough cover, made music when quarry was discovered, and the hawkers stood by ready to release their birds when it showed. 'The whole success of a day like this,' Laurie said, 'is plenty of quarry. With four hawks to keep busy, let's hope we see some.' In fact, we saw more than I would have believed possible with a small army such as ours present.

I learned that Harris's hawks will hunt together in harmony and that in fact they hunt as families in the wild. I was impressed by their obvious attachment to their owners and even more so by the way they worked with the dogs. It was quite astonishing. I have never seen its like before and have wondered ever since what I have been missing.

A rabbit bolted from rough cover into a thick hedgerow. I placed myself in the middle and turned it back towards the dogs. It broke for the open field eventually and the actual attack took place on the far side. It would seem that a second hawk came to the assistance of the first and that the final encounter took place on the far side of the hedgerow. The rabbit was confined to the game bag and the hunt continued.

At the edge of a rough hedge, where the ditch opened up into a small stream, the dogs went berserk, moorhens flew in all directions, and four hawks went to work with grace and precision. There was so much going on that I cannot record the events accurately, but I believe all four hawks accounted for their targets. In the midst of it all another rabbit bolted, and a partially distracted hawk took off after it. It missed by about a millimetre and the rabbit escaped. A cock pheasant broke from cover. Harriet took off after it but it had had too much of a start and she returned. A hare showed in the stubble, but two hawks could do little more than confuse it temporarily. That is one of the aspects of hawking that really appeals to me. I may be wrong, but it would appear that, like some other kinds of hunting, it is very much a case of hit or miss. The quarry is either killed or escapes unharmed; and I can find no fault in that.

Around the tree-fringed pond the hawkers released their birds and they immediately took up positions in the topmost branches. The dogs worked the muddy water and the bramble-covered banks, and mallard, which normally would have flown to safety, some-how seemed to sense the danger. They swam underwater, emerg-ing to take refuge in the thick cover until the dogs moved them again. And the very moment one of them showed itself to the hawks above, a sudden, silent, deadly dive from one of the trees spelt out its doom. Harriet took one almost at my feet, and I was then introduced to the subterfuge needed to coax a hawk off her prey. Placing a piece of rabbit meat strategically, Laurie swiftly and with great secrecy stole the mallard from his bird and slid it into the game bag.

Meanwhile, Griff's hawk had left her tree top and had flown to a nearby copse. Her owner went to seek her and returned with both her and her wood pigeon quarry. There were lots of feathers flying around, but the best was the one in Griff's cap. Wood pigeon are seldom caught by Harris's hawks, I understand.

The hawkers moved on; their hawks, seeing them depart, fol-lowed, and came to hand. A hen pheasant was added to the game bag somewhere along the line and, while wet hawks dried out and their owners partook of refreshment incredibly produced by Walter in his caravette in the middle of the afternoon, I eased my aching limbs and marvelled at it all.

With nineteen head of game accounted for, John said that we should settle for a final score of twenty. By that time I was past caring. My head was full of ideas, my mind was boggling, and I was as excited as a schoolboy.

'What about using ferrets to bolt rabbits for the hawks?' I asked.

'That's a great idea, boy,' said John. 'Trouble is the hawks sometimes catch more ferrets than rabbits!'

I got the message, but I still thought it would be fun.

In an incredibly thick area of dried-up swamp, covered with bracken, briars, thistles and tall grass, Laurie lofted his bird high while he walked through with a dog. Harriet dived in a sudden swoop and held down her quarry. Laurie eased her off and held it up.

'Ladies and gentlemen,' he reported. 'Quarry number twenty is a mouse!'

And that seemed to be as good a time as any to call it a day. It was a day I will *never* forget!

I had for years been involved in running a pheasant shoot of sorts and, when improved farming methods frustrated my attempts at holding birds because of lack of natural cover, my close shooting friends and I missed our weekly get-togethers. My first attempts at being an amateur keeper had met with incredible success (due largely to Lady Luck) since a run-down shoot had provided us with good sport for a number of years. Our shoots had eventually become little more than social meetings, but nevertheless we enjoyed our brief encounters with whatever came our way.

Always we were looking for something better, however, and it became almost an obsession with me to be part of a team dedicated to the building up of a shoot almost from scratch. Suddenly there came an opportunity. A big acreage of game country; a run-down shoot with great potential and a heap of problems. I walked a tiny corner of it to see signs of vermin and 'footpaths' that ought not to be there. I saw fantastic holding cover and the chance of sporting shots if all went well. I saw feeding as being easy, watering as being difficult, and all around me I saw neglect. I saw signs of deer, rabbit, pigeon in abundance, and some wild partridge coveys. And I was enthusiastic, even though I did not intend to be a full shooting member of the syndicate. More guns were invited to join and I offered to assist, when possible, in the day-to-day running of the shoot. I offered to help with the moving and building of pens, to pay irregular visits to deter unwanteds; to take my turn at feeding and to try and help keep down vermin. I also offered to beat on shooting days, and strangely enough I was not in the least envious of those who were to do the shooting. Somehow the driven bird was not for me, and my pleasure really lay in seeing ploys work successfully and in being able to witness good shots and retrieves.

The new shoot was not necessarily typical of a traditional driven pheasant shoot. There was more to it than that. It was in tough country, up hill and down dale, and the guns would have to work as hard as the rest. But there would be opportunities to take very high birds if ploys were successful. My companions had always welcomed such opportunities. I knew I was not a good enough shot to take advantage of them, and it suited me to play a supporting role.

In return there was rabbiting for me. I saw long netting, trapping, snaring, and rifle-shooting possibilities, though I had my doubts about ferreting. There were rabbit buries on those green hillsides and I thought it possible that some of them would respond to traditional ferreting with loose jills, but the great chunks of flint and limestone turned over by the plough made me cringe at the thought of digging. I had worked on nearby territory in years past and I could still feel the wrist-jarring thuds from the spade as I tried to peck away some of those boulders. Malcolm Baldwin and I had always been emphatic that any ferreted rabbits from that land were hard won. I saw no reason to believe that these would be any easier. Only time would tell, of course, and meanwhile there were working parties to be organized and plans for a thousand-bird-planting to be considered. I had only ever talked in terms of a hundred birds in the past, and the magnitude of it all excited me.

It took two hours of hard going to cover one corner of the shoot when I first walked it and even then I lost my sense of direction in the woodland. The smell of spruce was strong, the evening air was sweet and it brought back memories of other pine forests in hotter climes. A hundred pigeon clattered out of the trees, four pheasant (three hens and a cock bird) flushed in front as I walked the edge of the timber line. All were in shot. How often would such chances present themselves when the new season began, I wondered?

It was almost dark as I left and I reflected that I seldom went home with nothing to show for it when I took out my rifle. Tonight I was without food for the pot and my wife would tell me I was slipping.

Then, on the back road to the village a faster car overtook me – and I saw it brake suddenly and then proceed again. My headlights picked up a kicking body in the road and I stopped. A rabbit would no doubt be appreciated by the ferrets and I went to retrieve it. This was no rabbit, however, but a fine young jack hare. It had been killed by a hit on the head, and I tossed its carcase into the boot. It was completely unmarked and was later confined to the freezer to be transformed into pâté. I am not sure whether my wife credited my tale or not but, like me, she is a great believer in reaping nature's harvests – however strangely they are presented.

The opening of the new season was superb. With cooperation on all sides, advice from members of the adjoining shoot, and assistance from a very competent professional keeper, some magnificent sport evolved. I played my humble part as a beater and saw the results of my off-season cooperative labours in terms of high birds well presented and, in the main, well shot. I am in no doubt whatsoever, having had two invitations to shoot on what has now become a very high class operation, that I made the right choice. Those who shoot are still my very close and dear friends, and I believe they speak the truth when they say they have missed me on those days when I cannot attend to beat. But I believe I see more and learn more as I tap my way through the woods as a beater, trying hard to make the birds go the right way, than I would learn if I stood at a gun stand waiting for them to fly to their doom. I look forward to future seasons now with increased enthusiasm.

The Old Berkley Beagles were to meet at The Five Elms in Weedon, near to my home. Remembering the days when I had been a casual follower, I called in to see them and enjoy a lunchtime glass.

In the course of a conversation with a local villager, whom I knew only casually, the name of television personality Jack Hargreaves was mentioned. I had been involved with a few of Jack's fishing programmes in the past and I knew he had lived locally for a time, as the villager reminded me.

'Saw you on one or two of his programmes a few years ago,' he said. 'Wondered if he ever gets down this way. We remember him when he was at Burston up the road, you know. That was about fifty years ago, but we'd like to see him again.'

I promised to write to Jack and ask him if he would come to The Five Elms, his old local, for an evening. I ended the letter by saying that I'd done my part and that the rest was up to him. I knew him to be a busy man and I considered it highly unlikely that he would ever find the time to make such a trip. But Jack was enthusiastic.

'I never dreamed anyone would remember that far back,' he wrote. 'Yes, we will certainly get together.'

There was a long, long interval with odd letters passing between us from time to time and eventually we arranged to meet one evening and do a ferreting film for his programme the following day. After an evening spent in the local, we made the film at Manor Farm, Rowsham, with permission from Mr Fred Tofield, the owner.

The weather was kind, the sun shone, the ferrets behaved as always with diligence and charm. Rabbits bolted quickly and by lunchtime it was all 'in the can'. It was a nostalgic return for Jack, and an opportunity for Malcolm Baldwin and me to press home our feelings about gentle ferrets.

'They are a credit to you both,' Jack remarked before he left.

I recall Jack's visit with pleasure, since the film was very successful, but the highlight for me was a story Jack told in the local of his early days as a young veterinary student, living at Burston. He was, he said, rather shy and did not care much for big social gatherings, and was therefore a little confused when he was invited to an annual gathering of farmers and landlords at a grand hotel in Aylesbury.

He walked into the bar and blinked in the lamplight, looking hopefully for one familiar face.

'Ah,' said someone at the bar (who had better be known as Joe because that was his real name). 'Here's the young man from Burston. Tell me, young man, what are you doing with yourself these days?'

'Working,' said Jack.

'Don't work all the time do you?' asked Joe. 'What else do you get up to?'

'I ride the ponies a bit,' Jack replied.

'Yes, I've seen you about from time to time,' Joe allowed. 'What else?'

'I shoot a bit,' said Jack.

'Oh,' said Joe. 'Got a gun then, 'ave you?'

'Yes,' replied Jack. 'I've got an old twenty-bore single barrel.'

'Twenty-bore,' mused Joe. 'That's a pretty odd sort of a gun. Can you get cartridges for it?'

'Oh yes,' Jack assured him. 'They've got plenty in the shop in Kingsbury Square.'

'Ah,' said Joe. 'I know the ones you mean. Little yeller beggars, ain't they?'

'That's right,' replied Jack. 'Little yellow ones.'

'Well, you must be the only bloke around here buying them kind of cartridges I reckon, ain't you?' asked Joe in a friendly tone.

'Could be, I suppose,' said Jack.

'That's what I thought,' said Joe, and putting his hand in his pocket pulled out an empty, yellow, twenty-bore case. 'So what the 'ell was this doin' on *my* land?'

There is no real answer to that! But Jack, it seems, told Joe he had shot a pigeon and it had fallen over the boundary. He went to pick it up and must only then have broken his gun.

'That'll do, I suppose,' said Joe. 'What do you want to drink?'

It was a lovely story; one that took me back to the days when I had used the same excuse myself less than a mile from where we sat. . . .

So what, now, are my thoughts of the future?

Field sportsmen and good conservation have truly ensured that game is plentiful in this country. Britain is still the Mother Country of game shooters, as many visiting sportsmen readily concede, and (despite the attitude of many ill-informed 'antis') it happens to be a fact that sporting husbandry has ensured the reproduction of many endangered species. Without the shooter there would be no pheasants in this country and the native grey partridge would have been extinct.

I respect the person who is genuinely opposed to hunting, shooting and fishing for emotional and/or religious reasons, provided he or she is well informed. I have no time, however, for saboteurs whose only aims are to disrupt and make political capital.

I have always believed that nature provides a crop for us to harvest and that it is wasteful not to reap it. I believe also that it is sinful to over-crop, and in the shooting field I am convinced that a superb balance has been established. It has been done without legislation or limits, through the deep understanding of field sportsmen in general.

I have no doubt that, given good health, my shooting, ferreting, beating, trapping, netting, snaring and fishing will continue. And I am convinced that, because I wish to continue those practices, I shall never be the cause of shortages. Myxomatosis could not wipe out the rabbits in the 1950s (though it was a very close thing) and I am quite certain that nothing I can do will exterminate them. I take a crop, a large crop, every winter, and I shoot with my rifle often during the summer months at selected targets. I keep numbers down to a tolerable level, but that is all.

Wood pigeons suffered tremendous losses during the prolonged freeze of 1963, but they are back again in large numbers. They are shot and harried quite ruthlessly by shooters all over the country, but each year they breed and multiply. Nature and the crops men grow assure their future and provide a harvest of food that has to be reaped. Without pigeon shooters and rabbit hunters, our own farm crops would suffer and other methods would have to be found to protect them. Poisons and gases provide the only other possible answers to those problems. The creatures would have to die regardless, but in those circumstances there would be no return. Their carcases would be inedible and it would be a wasteful exercise.

More and better farming methods have destroyed the habitat of some of our game birds, but the surplus grain left behind by modern combining methods helps to feed the reared birds put down by shooting men each year. Today there is more interest in shooting and game birds are almost certainly more numerous and widespread than ever before.

In my youth I never saw, nor even hoped to see, a deer of any kind in my native Buckinghamshire. Now they are commonplace; their numbers have reached problem proportions in some timbered country.

Trout fishing has improved beyond bounds due to the splendid conservation policies of trout anglers, trout farmers and those responsible for certain still-water environments. Rainbow trout, reared and stocked on a put-and-take basis, provide sport and good food for anglers, and the offshoot from it all has meant that trout can now be purchased at a modest price for the table. The great strides made in the conversion of protein pellets into edible pink flesh have helped to supplement our diminishing sea returns. The future in all those respects seems healthy enough and I believe my larder will always remain well stocked through my sporting activities.

The only real dark spots are the continued pollution, abstraction and dredging of our rivers. Very few rivers remain pure enough to support trout; many of those having annual runs of salmon have deteriorated badly over the past twenty years, and I do not know of one river where the coarse fishing has improved or even remained up to par, though certain still waters have produced coarse fish of a size that was unheard of a quarter of a century ago. When Richard Walker and I, in the 1950s, mentioned tench in the double-figure bracket, most of the angling world fell about laughing. Today the record stands at over ten pounds. Bream weighing over ten pounds are now fairly commonplace, and no one raises an eyebrow when yet another thirty-pound carp is reported. One explanation for this kind of explosion is the use of modern fertilizers which have leached into some of those waters noted for their big fish.

Redmire pool has always been a big fish water because the balance is somehow right. The water is extremely fertile (possibly due to the seepage of cow manure from the nearby farm, though I have no knowledge of the present-day situation) but it is (or was) pumped to the nearby village for drinking water. This also applies to some of the larger still waters and reservoirs around the country, and for that very reason there is no danger of pollution. We should, at least, give thanks for that.

I still regard myself as a coarse fisherman and I look forward each season to my tench, carp and pike fishing, but the sport has indeed seen a lot of changes. Sometimes, when I look at the waters I used to fish, and where I used to swim and dive when I fancied, I despair. Today I could paddle across some of them in bedroom slippers without getting wet feet. In my youth I caught pound roach and perch there with crude tackle and little angling skill.

The dredger has again passed through our once lovely upper Great Ouse reach, leaving behind an eyesore and an utterly ruined fishery. The last time the river was dredged we were assured (but did not for one moment believe) that it would bring about an improvement. In fact a survey carried out showed that the average size and numbers of fish are well down. When I think back to the days of those five-pound chub, those three-pound perch and occasional two-pound roach, I am truly on the verge of tears.

I am not pro-otter hunting, despite my hunting instincts. I have my reasons, which I will not go into, but in the past I have been privileged to see the odd otter on the upper reaches of that river. Even when I have not seen the animals, I have often recognized their signs. Today they are gone, and I see no hopes of their return. I can see little future for coarse fishing as I always knew it.

My thoughts take these lines whenever I find myself retracing the paths of my youth in order to see what really has happened to some of the waters I used to fish. The Meeting of the Waters is still there. Or at least the two muddy ditches where the so-called waters meet are. I cannot believe there are any real fish present; they would be hard put to find breathing space now. But at one time the waters met and formed a great wide confluence where lilies flourished on two banks and a lively current encouraged shoals of fine roach and dace.

It is hard to believe that the Oxhouse Corner, now little more than a muddy puddle, used to be a favourite pike and perch hole. I once saw a perch of almost three pounds come from the old Oxhouse Corner, and as a boy I can remember seeing a local butcher haul out two huge pike (about fifteen pounds and twelve pounds respectively) on live roach baits fished below a gaudy bung and a string of pilots. I remember the incident well because he threatened to box my ears if I did not keep quiet. I was young then and had little thought for the stealthy approach. That came later in my life.

I recall how we used to swim under the road bridge and collect caddis grubs for bait, chuck them out on improvised outfits and leave them to fish for themselves. When we tired of swimming, we would go back to the tackle and lift out a big roach or a baitless hook, depending on how fortune had smiled upon us. Now the very sight of the road bridge pool depresses me, and I wish we might have done something about it. My generation and the one before it were involved in wars and poverty, however, and we had no real opportunity to make our voices heard. It was probably our own fault, and had we been as wise then as we profess to be now, our kids might still be enjoying the fishing we did. We let it slip through our fingers but, on reflection, I wonder what we could have done.

We had our fishing too cheaply for too long. We know that now, but even had we realized it all those years ago, I doubt very much if we could have done much about it. We simply could not have afforded to fish if the real value of the fisheries had been asked. It is easy enough to talk about our heritage and our God-given rights, and about the rivers belonging to everyone, but it does not always work out that way. This country is too small for free-for-alls, and if we want to fish and enjoy good fishing, we shall have to pay for it. Most of us recognize that fact now, but I still wonder if it is enough.

I wonder, too, if we coarse fish anglers ourselves are not to blame for some of the deterioration of our fisheries. The practice of catching fish and leaving them to die and rot on the bank has, thankfully, long since been discontinued, but I wonder if we are achieving anything worthwhile by returning *everything* we catch at the end of the day as we do now.

In the distant past we killed fish unnecessarily; today we kill nothing – or next to nothing. We return badly conditioned fish religiously season after season, and we leave them to breed more badly conditioned fish. If the truth be told, many of our coarse fishing waters are grossly overstocked and badly need thinning out, but the thought of killing and eating some of the fish from them is very much frowned upon by the average coarse fish angler. We have been somehow brainwashed into believing that it is right to return fish and evil to kill them. When perch were plentiful and I was lucky enough to catch a netful, I often selected three weighing about a pound apiece to take home at the end of the day. The remainder I returned to the water. Once or twice, every year, I would take away a few fillets for the pan, firstly because I enjoyed them, and secondly because I always felt that I should maintain my right to do so. I enjoy catching and eating trout and no one would expect me to return these to the water; so why should I not do the same occasionally with perch? I would still make a point of catching and eating them today if there were any left to take from the waters I fish.

I also note an air of secrecy and suspicion growing up between coarse fishermen. They, who were once referred to as 'brothers of the angle', have now become super-cautious. Many are only interested in how much can be made in the shape of prize money, pools and returns from the bookmaker. I think back to the days when members of the Carp Catchers' Club were falling over themselves to pass on snippets of information that might help their fellow men catch more or bigger carp. I remember the days when the Tenchfishers' Club did the same sort of thing. We fished then for the joy of fishing, and of seeing another angler do as well as we did. It was a great day for us when one of our 'pupils' beat the 'master'. Today it would seem to be almost a crime in some circles.

A few summers ago, a young friend of mine, Steve, went carp fishing for the first time in his life, under the guidance of a more experienced carp man. It bored him, he said, because he preferred a more active type of fishing, but by patience and sheer luck he caught a twenty-pounder. His 'tutor' was delighted, as indeed I would have been myself, but there were others close by who were not so pleased.

'I don't suppose you would care to tell me what bait you were using,' asked one – obviously expecting a refusal. Steve, having always been associated with the 'open mind' school, was astonished.

'Certainly,' he replied. 'I caught it on a lump of trout pellet paste.'

'Is it your first twenty-pounder?'

'Mate,' said Steve, 'it's my first ever!'

That ended the conversation. Steve, it seemed, was not one to be encouraged. This tyro had not put in the hours and did not know the jargon; and not being one of the regulars, he did not warrant further interest. I find it hard to believe that such attitudes exist, but they do. I can hardly believe that one angler would not be delighted at another's good fortune, but it seems those sporting feelings have gone by the board in recent years. We kept no secrets. We shared our thoughts regarding baits and methods. Today, special baits are treated with great secrecy and it is laughable that some of them derive from baits and information brought back from the USA and published by me years ago.

I remember those mad and glorious days during the 1950s and 1960s when we cleared our swim and baited it down, knowing full well that it would be respected as ours. No one else would dream of moving in to fish it. We had prepared it; it would be ours to fish next day and we knew it. Every so often I try to relive those days. I still have the use of a pontoon boat and just once or twice a season, perhaps, I stay out overnight in that glorious Sawmills lake at Wotton and listen to the sounds of the night. With my deck chair on its lowest notch, the canopy pulled over to conserve the warmth of the little tea-brewing stove, and an ungodly amount of warm clothing, I doze away the dark hours. It is still magic and, although I do not catch the fish I used to catch and despite my misgivings about coarse fishing generally, I know that I can still look forward to some of the magic there each summer.

When the first hints of autumn arrive with the end of the trout season, my lightweight spinning rods, nets, and guns will come out of retirement once more. Throughout the winter I shall fish for my pike, hunt my rabbits, shoot my hares, pheasant and pigeon, and hopefully continue to provide for my needs and the needs of my family.

The open fire in my small bungalow will burn brightly while the wind howls outside and I decide whether or not to run my long net in the dark. My wife's 'cellar' is stocked to capacity with those wines of the countryside she has made over the past few years, and her larder shelves are loaded with preserves made from wild fruits and berries. From being a town person she has become a knowledgeable lover of the countryside, and all that it has to offer. Our cups are almost full to overflowing, but still the tiny town of Wanneroo beckons. . . .

Afterword

Wanneroo is now no longer a tiny town but a recognised Australian city. It seems impossible that I have been back there ten times since this book was first completed!

It still beckons and will continue to do so but, in the meantime, there are other wild and desolate outbacks to visit and explore. I have re-discovered Canada and its magnificent wilderness areas, and I yearn to see again the snows of Manitoba and the fly-ridden lakes of The Northwest Territories. I plan to catch a sturgeon from the Red River and a truly monstous eel from New Zealand. So much to do; so many places yet to visit.

My sporting and outdoor life did not stop when this book was first published. If anything, my activities have since increased and my life, though lived at a slower pace, has been enriched as a result.

Fred J. Taylor
July 1997